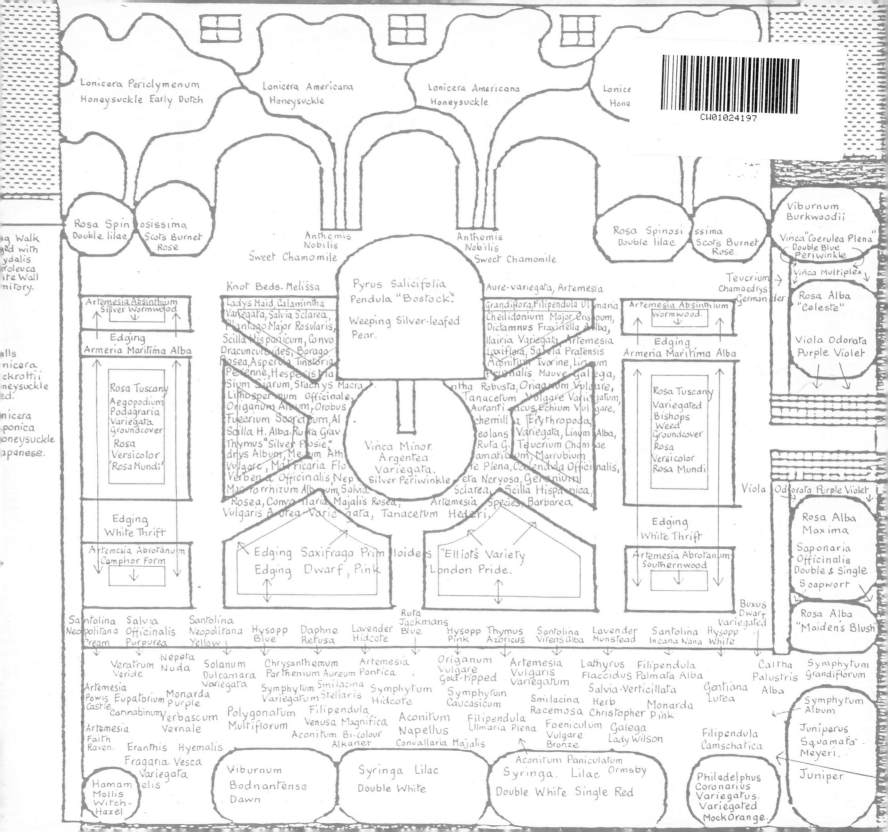

HERTERTON HOUSE AND A NEW COUNTRY GARDEN

FRANK LAWLEY

HERTERTON HOUSE AND A NEW COUNTRY GARDEN

The story of how an ancient house
was brought back to life and
a fitting garden created around it

WITH PHOTOGRAPHY BY VAL CORBETT

For Marjorie

HERTERTON HOUSE AND A NEW COUNTRY GARDEN

A catalogue record for this book is available from the British Library.

ISBN 978 1 9102 5858 3

Designed by Zinco Design
Typeset in Gill Sans Alt One MT Book
Printed and bound in China
10 9 8 7 6 5 4 3 2 1

Inside front and back cover: details of Marjorie's plans; red and pastel beds (left) and pink and cream beds (right).
Page i: the Physic Garden
Page ii: the old house seen from the meadow, framed by wild alders along the river edges.
Page iv: a pair of Scottish stone urns mark the entrance to the flower garden.
Page v: one of Marjorie's hen drawings.

CONTENTS

FOREWORD

I first heard of Frank and Marjorie Lawley's miraculous garden at Herterton when Penguin Books published *The Englishman's Garden* in 1982. I marvelled at their ability to grow so many interesting plants in the harsh Northumberland uplands that I had known in my own teenage years at nearby Kirkharle. The garden was only six years old then, so it was clear that the book's editors, Alvilde Lees-Milne and Rosemary Verey, had formed a very high opinion of the quality and importance of what had already been achieved. And it was evident that Frank was an intelligent, sensitive and fluent writer.

Ten years later, when I began to edit the Royal Horticultural Society's Yearbook and Garden Finder, I made my first visit to Herterton. The garden had grown up since 1982 and it was the structure, rather than the flowers, that then made the greatest impression on me. I realised that it was the quiet, orderly design, as much as the plantings, that created its spirit of peace and orderliness. Further visits revealed the unity and harmony that the Lawleys established between the house, the garden, its plantings and the wider landscape. Only recently did I realise that this unity applied equally to the restoration and furnishing of the house.

This book tells the story from Herterton's earliest days, tracing the influences and experiences that guided the Lawleys' developing ideas of garden design and planting. They were fortunate to live at Wallington, which had for many years been a centre for high culture under the progressive ownership of the Trevelyan family and, later, of the National Trust. The 'Wallington experience' was crucial, not just as a catalyst for the Lawleys' development as artists and gardeners, but also for its devotion to Fabianism and the Arts and Crafts movement. Frank maintains that he and Marjorie have always been fortunate to be 'in the right place at the right time', but it should also be said that they were the right people to be there. Their sensibilities, their education and their curiosity helped them to benefit enormously from what surrounded them at Wallington and from what they encountered on their travels to other parts of Britain.

The Lawleys rented Herterton – they still do – from the National Trust. Making the garden was preceded by lengthy years of planning, tempered by self-discipline and exercised with restraint. The many tasks of restoration and building were imbued with a reverence for the skills and achievements of craftsmen. And the Lawleys were interested in the history of plants – the horticultural pedigrees of the plants they acquired – as well as their beauty and usefulness to mankind.

This is an important book, testimony to the Lawleys' aesthetic education and their acquisition of learning. It is the story of two lives spent making and maintaining an exceptional garden, an outstanding work of art, a paragon where design, artistry and horticulture are perfectly blended. Frank Lawley understands line and structure, light and shadow, colour and texture. Time and again his use of language – so observant, so poetic and so accurate – takes one's breath away.

Herterton still belongs to the National Trust. It is to be hoped that the Trust will recognise what a remarkable work of art its tenants have created and devote itself to conserving Herterton exactly as the Lawleys have made it. Certainly, this book supplies a full apologia to guide the Trust in understanding the origins of both the house and the garden, and in maintaining both in the future. It is a monument to a garden, a house, a way of life and a system of values that hold together with complete integrity. It will come to be seen as a masterpiece of garden-writing that places Frank Lawley among the greatest of horticultural authors and, jointly with Marjorie, among the greatest of English garden-makers.

Charles Quest-Ritson

Following page: trug with peony seedpods.

LOOKING FORWARD

This is the second garden my wife Marjorie and I have made, and should you think that practice makes perfect, or that second ones are bound to be easier than first ones, this account may be a surprise. It may even serve as a warning that, if you are not careful, gardening can take over your life.

A search has been made through our memories for indications of motivation. Why gardening, when we might have been doing something else? Why here; why bother with such a ruined place when it must have been so clear to everyone else that the place was simply not worth bothering about? Yet life seems most enjoyable when you are bothering about something and are fully engaged on the spot with whatever is at hand. A simple record of having done this and then that, and of having used this and that plant, would be an artificial formula if no further reasons were provided. It would leave us out of the picture. Plans and diagrams arise out of feelings, and these are generated from past experiences, some of which reach back to early times. Therefore, it seems that we are indispensible and so an element of biography is included.

The book divides into four parts. 'The Apprenticeship' begins with early memories, observations and encounters which have not been forgotten, and now seem relevant to the story. There is some account of our 'wilderness' years when, after our union, we set out modestly to travel to discover the island we belonged to, and which we found to be perfectly adequate. Our vision is undoubtedly insular and provincial and simple, but it has provided fully the stimulus we have required to come to feel able to take part in the culture and to try to contribute ourselves.

We had received good educations which have served us extremely well, but we did not emerge with the label of a profession pinned to our jackets. Our specialist studies were in art, during which no one had ever mentioned the art of gardening. But within a year or two of beginning to make our first cottage garden, we most unexpectedly found ourselves irrevocably committed to gardening. We had found that it had a lot in common with art. Making a garden provided an opportunity to compose and plan, as you could on a canvas on an easel. An enticing new vision emerged of working on this much larger scale, which added the extra dimensions of time and space.

However, gradually conviction grew that it was necessary for us to start again, because our first garden had not been composed from the outset and in addition its size came to feel inadequate. Whether you are a miniaturist or a mover of landscapes, there is a scale for everyone, which must be discovered.

Much inspiration was derived from living for thirteen years, as and where we did, in that cottage on the National Trust Wallington estate in Northumberland. This was formerly the home of the Trevelyan family, known nationally as historians, politicians and patrons of the arts. So the second part of the book, called 'Taking Stock', assesses how dynamic this apparently quietest of places actually was.

There, we lived between three cultures. Lady Trevelyan still lived in the great house and with the aid of her ploughman, her shepherd and her farm manager maintained the home farm. The village culture, too, was then still intact. Neighbours spoke of 'us'ns' and 'them'ns' just as Flora Thompson had described so faithfully in 1945 in *Lark Rise to Candleford*. They knew about townies but they were simply irrelevant. Then, after the death of Lady T (as she was commonly called in the local vernacular) we watched the coming of a new order, introduced by the National Trust.

When we moved to Wallington in 1964 we found, wherever we looked, how busily everyone worked and with what conviction and pleasure. There were many experts in many fields, valuing excellence, and this included both visualising and making. Some people think most clearly when actually doing a job; this is the art of the artisan, which is much the same for some artists too. Their best thoughts are generated in that way. It was very stimulating, the busyness was infectious; we came to want to do more rather than less. Working days stretched to 9 p.m. and fifty years later still do.

We would approach our task differently at Hartington. Having thrown ourselves into our first encounter, we intended to meet the second one with a much surer vision of what we wished to create. Our assessment of the possibilities is recalled in detail, including the discussion of probable limitations and restrictions. Hartington offered the right scale, and an excitingly different cultural and physical environment.

The third part, 'The New Garden', is the history of how the garden was made, and how our initial thoughts about its design were adapted to its actual situation. Each aspect of the work, including the selection of plants, the order of their planting and how they were to be maintained, necessitated the invention of new techniques and methods, which could not have been imagined in advance. Ideas were stretched and bent by what seemed a very unsympathetic environment, but we came to accept the modifications imposed by the climate as positive elements: partners in defining the particular character of the garden which has evolved. It is remarkable to discover what can be done if it has to be done and how absorbing it is to do it: and what a delight to meet the craftsmen whose contributions of might and insight are now everywhere reflected.

Making a garden here should really have been much too daunting a prospect, but we are not professional designers who might have asked quite different questions about the site. We certainly came to appreciate how choice the situation of our first garden had been; it had sheltering woods and ancient black garden soil. But while Hartington had severe brutal limitations, we discovered that it also seemed to possess a magic which came to our aid. So many new helpful faces, and even one ghost emerged, while many of the old ones fell away. Although we had to make many decisions about new problems we had not faced before, we seemed to be propelled forwards. The dilemmas are discussed and explanation offered for the choices we made.

The new garden is much larger than the first. Working on a new scale was a challenge. Progress was sometimes halted; two major alterations had to be made to the euphoric plan drawn in 1975. Fortunately the first problem was recognised quickly and its solution seen at the same time. However, the second, also soon recognised, was not solved permanently for a long time, though a useful temporary solution was found. Then, after the long delay, an inspiration one afternoon resolved the matter entirely to our satisfaction.

The final part is 'Reinventing the House'. The house was at the beginning of the story, and it has been a passionate concern all along. The book allots three-quarters of its space to the garden and one-quarter to the house. These proportions reflect the time we have actually devoted to the two parts of our lives. The house has been a private retreat where it may be true that some cobwebs stretch from March to October. We have neither a reserve staff of gardeners nor one of house carers.

We loved the house before we ever considered making a garden here. It was a small anonymous place whose identity was in danger of being lost for ever as a sacrifice to progress. While progress is important, we are so pleased that this unassuming old house has been saved. It has magically recovered its known losses and, we trust, its due dignity and now has a garden as compensation for having lost its farm. Charles Paget Wade of Snowshill Manor, who appears in the last chapter, rescued a mountain of treasures, while our contribution is just one house to which we have fitted a garden. Thanks to all the curious looking and searching we did half a century ago, we were able to discover that Herterton is our sort of place, our little niche in the world. We can identify with it.

The final chapter looks at how the interior has been furnished. Furnishings are discussed in the same way as the plants which furnished the garden, and there is a guided tour. And the question of whether the inside is in harmony with what is outside is raised too.

We would like to think that the combination of house and garden may have achieved that sense of contented union, including union with the landscape, which was so striking wherever we came upon such anonymous places in the countryside. Their timeless sense of belonging made them the ideal house of 'Mr Nobody of Nowhere', which seemed just right. Great people are known to come from great houses although that is not always the case. The first nudge towards finding how we might fit into the world came with the discovery of those old places in Stratford described in the first part. Consider who came from there. ('Mr Nobody' is in the outstanding collection of English pottery in the Fitzwilliam Museum, and he is clearly a villain. He is responsible for all the otherwise inexplicable damages which occur in your home. Neither I nor you could possibly be blamed. Actually he is only an ancient legend.) And this book now reveals for a moment just who the present Mr and Mrs Nobody who live at Herterton actually are.

Inevitably we have met and visited other gardeners, some now legends with a place in history books. They had homes too, for a garden is not a garden without a home, and so I have revealed details of some of those visits, which were memorable in themselves and may also have provided us with both reassurances and ambitions.

Following page: the Northumbrian 'yellow' snowdrop.

Part One

THE APPRENTICESHIP

SOMEWHERE ELSE

Barely half a mile from home in Staffordshire, at the foot of a steep hill where everyone came after snow for sledging and sliding, was a small half-timbered farmhouse. This was Arch's Farm. It stood discreetly back from the narrow lane in a low walled farmyard, with a magnificent chestnut tree in the front corner. Stables and barn joined on, and a high round-topped barn of colourful corrugated iron gave some height to the group. Behind, the flank of the hill gave shelter.

Here, between 1950 and 1954, I painted at least half a dozen watercolours: just the house, the house and the lane and the chestnut, the house and its buildings in the landscape. Once, Mrs Arch came out to me and asked if I would like to see inside. This was a great shock and surprise, but it was polite to say 'Yes'. I would love to go inside, but I was desperately shy. It might have seemed almost rude to look up from the floor. I now wonder what I saw.

I also painted the cornfield with its pyramid stooks, and the cream painted inn just past the chestnut tree. I often walked the path over the steeply rising ploughed field where I sometimes met Uncle 'lijah on his way to look after someone's pigeons nearby. At the inn another lane turned left and passed two abandoned old houses. The one along a track on the right made a wonderful sight with the first flush of spring green and an angry purple sky behind. It was said that Purcell had once lived in the one on the left. This was now so overwhelmed by its trees and vegetation that no young explorer needed to pass the remains of the Keep Out sign. It could have been full of ghosts! A little further, the scramble of silver birches lining the lane opened into a clearing. Here from time to time the gypsies came. Their lovely caravans, well spaced, made a miniature village green. Their 'transports' enjoyed the grass. I liked to walk by discreetly. I longed to see into these elegant interiors through the small shaped and painted doorways that were raised so comfortably high above the ground, but I knew that one should not stare. The ladies brought baskets of homemade pegs to furnish our washing lines. We used to buy some.

Before 1960, the old farm had vanished. Everywhere old houses and cottages were being condemned. Often, having stamped earth floors, they were damp. Long before, Baring Gould, in his *Old Country Life* of 1889, had written passionately that the old clay mortars gave the perfect water seal, but was he right? People wanted to have bathrooms, and bedrooms with 'flat tops' (ceilings). This would be so much better for the spring clean whitewash than the beams, thirsty for linseed oil, and the 'T-foils' and small gabled windows. Once condemned, as if criminals, there was little hope of survival.

At Arch's, three miles from their offices, the local town council saw a wonderful opportunity for development. Fields could provide terraces and avenues, and carefully placed, new high-rise blocks – a celebration of concrete – could give some distinction to that rural landscape. It would be a clear message to all who approached this town of its commitment to the future.

New communities might not need space or gardens, but they would need good public transport, which then meant trolley buses and electric wires. Somewhere where the inn was, a traffic island would be needed to get all comfortably into the gypsies' lane. Or, would the chestnut tree make a good traffic island?

No trace was left of 'old Arch's' and its quiet corner of the world. The loss was deeply felt. I still haven't returned to see the development.

At Wallington, the great estate owner, Sir Charles Trevelyan, faced the condemnation of a typical early Northumbrian low stone-slated cottage with an outside stone staircase to small attics. It was sheltered by eighteenth-century woods at the end of the north drive from the great house. It was very damp, etc., etc. I don't know what he could have said, but it is still there and smiles when you pass on the way to the village.

Marjorie was born just across the road in a row of four cottages. She came to know and love the interior of that little survivor. She still talks of the oak coffer with its garnish of peonies from the garden.

By 1975 we had spent twelve years in Marjorie's birth cottage. In 1970 a very successful partnership with the National Trust had seen it joined to its equally small neighbour to our own design. Before this, we had known damp and the inconvenience of not having a bathroom. We had a tin 'bungalow' bath, and made trips over the communal backyard, through the snow, to the WC. At that time, the planners said that you needed to have three bedrooms before a bathroom was allowed. There seemed to be a conspiracy against the improvement of small homes.

Now, on a lovely summer morning, I sat in the estate office. The estate had become a very flourishing and creative National Trust estate, said to be the largest in England. I had come to ask the agent if there was somewhere else where we could start again.

We did not want to leave the estate where we seemed to know everyone, and where Marjorie's mother, now widowed, lived in the courtyard busily and happily involved with Trevelyans and National Trust alike. Our nursery plants were selling very well in the new courtyard shop. And Marjorie was beginning to feel the need to become something of a mother to her mother. But urgently we needed to make a new and larger garden, designed from the outset, where we could receive visitors.

It was a very serious question. It was answered in a very creative and proper way . . . 'Well, have you ever considered the old place at Hartington?'

It was in the making of our first garden that a completely unanticipated passion for gardening had overwhelmed our lives. That garden of about a quarter of an acre was made by joining the two narrow strips in front of the two cottages which themselves had now been joined and turned into one. It sloped down to a low wall and a wood. This wood was part of a great eighteenth-century garden which swept gradually down and round to the river, with its fine bridge, in front of Wallington House. At the side of the cottage we had rented another strip of land to make a nursery garden. The farmer did not really miss this for it was 'spoilt' by a great oak tree. Its only use had been to provide a resting place for rusty old pieces of equipment. Also, independently, we had managed to rent an unwanted vegetable allotment. The rent was a promise to cut a very small lawn through the season.

In 1982, writing my chapter for the book *The Englishman's Garden*, I remembered beginning. 1964 seemed to have been a long and lovely summer stretching until October. The soil was old black garden soil, evidence that there had been older cottages there before. However, since no one had wanted to live there for a while, it had not been worked. The best part, at the top of the slope, had been put to use as a young tree nursery by the estate woodmen. The trees were growing well, but woodmen have no time for weeding. After the trees were taken away, we could start.

Every weed was taken out, and the soil was raked and levelled. How energetic we were, and how we loved our work. Looking back I saw myself as a sundial, the only feature in the garden. The shadow of my head slowly moved around my feet on the warm dry soil as the mornings became afternoons, and the afternoons became evenings.

Sometimes in the evening, we enjoyed the luxury of a short local ride in our first car, a Morris Minor. We enjoyed looking at the varied flora of different lanes. As we gradually came to know garden flowers, we took greater interest in the wild ones. The publication of 'Keble Martin' (the Revd William Keble Martin's *Concise British Flora in Colour*) made life even richer.

Hartington was three miles away; we always liked that lane. It had flowers, willows and houses. A mile long, it connects two small roads going to Rothbury. Useful to local people, it is unknown to the rest of the world.

We often started at the east end. Past the copse and over a little humpy bridge the flowers began. In the last shady bit of verge, close to the burn, wood cranesbill came and the melancholy thistle. Then bluebells spread into the sun with wood anemones and cowslips. Later when grasses are high and coarse, pride of place goes to the greater burnet. Its mysterious burgundy-brown thimbles stand above a great jostle of meadowsweet and umbellifers, but it is well camouflaged.

There seemed to be just one bush of the willow with small grey leaves tucked into the hawthorns, and you only saw the magnificent white willow if you knew when and where to look. As the road suddenly ducks under the railway bridge – its track is now part of a network of National Trust walks – for a second you need to look the wrong way. If in that moment you look above and behind the bridge it is there.

The next section of the lane has an avenue of ash trees. Last into leaf, and first out, they are a glorious yellow in the autumn. But the first of the frosts brings the leaves down. There are ditches either side, the very dykes that February fills! Under one ash tree, facing south, great clumps of white violets cling just below the coarse grass.

The avenue ends when a narrow track turns right and climbs steeply to a ridge with four houses. That is High Hartington. And quite suddenly you are into Hartington itself. The hamlet has five houses.

You would probably pass the first two. A fine Georgian house lies back surrounded by trees and walls and a track of laurels, and its cottage is sheltered by a handsome old cherry tree to one side and a dark bulging holly on the other. But you will be looking at a tall three-storied house which seems to have almost grown out of the road. This is the 'Hall'. Dutifully the road bends a little in passing, then, respectfully standing back, is the old place I had now been asked to consider. At its west end a long low byre was added, then two small farm cottages.

'Just drive in, round to the back. You'll know Bert, and old Bill . . .' Everyone knew Bert. He was the retired, never-to-be-replaced butcher who had called at everyone's door twice a week. He had found great pleasure in moving out of the village and making a home out of the little farm cottages.

Old Bill was less well known. He had spent his life with an elder, now dead, brother and his sister farming 'out on the hills'. Retirement had been accepted at 80, and when the Hall ceased to be a farm, perhaps in 1959, they had moved in with generations of family furniture. The land passed on to two farmer neighbours. Only the acre of unwanted farmyard, a barn and an open arched granary and the 'old place' stood empty.

We had often seen old Bill when we passed. He was always 'about the place'. Just as some people are said to have houses that don't get dirty and are always neat and tidy, Bill had one of those gardens where weeds don't grow. His grass was cut; there was a show of bright flowers, good vegetables and a perfect drying green. And after he had put the two cats to bed in the old pigsty – always with their saucers at 6 p.m. (they were waiting at the door) – he had time to sit on his small bench against the garden wall until the sun was lost in treetops. We are always 'about' in our garden, too.

Long ago Marjorie had made a note from one of those old gardening books (Alfred Austin's *The Story of my Garden*) which promised that you can tell what sort of people may live in a house by the state of their garden.

Another surprise when you reach the hamlet is the sudden appearance of the river just over the road. It has come charging in from the west end of the lane, almost touching the road at one point. This is the Hart of Hartington, or, properly, the Hart Burn. In front of the houses in its sunken basin it makes a fine bend by the old stepping stones, then races away. And I now know that if you should look out of a tiny bedroom window on a clear night, you might see an astonishing light in the water as it reflects a full moon. On many a summer afternoon, its chattering waters will be the only sound you will hear.

On our journeys, we had often paused to look at that old place. Its rugged masonry was like that of the Hall, very different from the other estate houses, which were mostly Victorian. In the 1890s a great Trevelyan improver, making his modern ideal estate, employed fine masons to create slight Cotswold charm. This was a typical longhouse, farmer at one end, beast at the other. It was probably Tudor like the Hall, whose good order had been noted in a border survey of about 1540.

Had it survived because the Hall was a listed building, the dower house to Wallington, or because the farmer who moved in during the early eighteenth century came to devise a new purpose for it (it became a byre)? Clearly it was the only house that had avoided improvement at a later stage. The great eighteenth-century building surge had spread from Wallington to all parts, and had given the Hall a more Georgian appearance and had put the new barn and the handsome open arched granary behind the longhouse.

It quite seriously lacked good order! Would it have survived the damp test? Its north wall was not just green, it was black! No one had repaired its roof for untold years. Even the acre was degraded. Foundations of a corrugated iron barn remained, a homemade concrete road curled across, a partly fallen wall stood at a very odd angle, happy new ash trees sprouted from drains, weeds were prolific and unknown passers-by had left other things . . .

Now thoughts had to be thought. Measurements, drawings, and financial searches made. Close relatives were appalled. But its size and position were perfect. And when you are 38, you can, of course, do anything. Our answer had to be 'Yes'. And, Hartington was beautiful. It was another 'Arch's'. It needed to recover due dignity, and it needed a new country garden.

At last the agent was able to draw up a lease and then one problem remained. If the old place had once had a name, history had not recorded it. However, I had by then looked into John Hodgson's *History of Northumberland*, published in 1827, in which he explained that before Hartington had become the hamlet's rightful name there were several other versions, including 'Herterton'. To save the postman headaches, the house was christened Herterton House, in deference to neighbouring Hartington Hall. Colloquially, the name has become simply Herterton.

One afternoon, after we had begun the first job, that of uprooting the deeply stoned muck-midden in front of the house, an old retired farmer visiting Bill paused for a moment. He was said to be a 'nice' farmer, and he spoke in a friendly if wistful way . . . 'Ah, hinny, but ye'll nivver make a garden here . . .' He didn't live to see the formal garden now there. And over the years since we began, one or two other people called to see what we have been doing. The agent had offered them the same opportunity. He had been trying to get rid of his 'old place' for at least ten years before our conversation in 1975. Everyone had turned it down; they told us their stories. Among them was Michael Tooley. He was engaged in a voluntary mission to recreate the then entirely lost little garden Gertrude Jekyll had designed for Edward Hudson beside Lindisfarne Castle. His devotion to her work was clear when, with his wife Rosanna, he published *The Gardens of Gertrude Jekyll in Northern England* in 1982, to coincide with the fiftieth anniversary of her death. But he, like the others, was not impressed by the 'old place'.

Left: Frank painting in the lane leading to Arch's Farm in the early 1950s.
Above: the finished painting.

Arch's Farm and the chestnut tree (early 1950s).

The cottage at Wallington which escaped condemnation, and the row of cottages in which Marjorie was born (1960).

SOMETHING FOR US TO DO

When Betty came downstairs after giving birth to Marjorie, her third child, she found a posy of double white primroses laid just inside her open front door; this had been left by her old neighbour. It was Easter Sunday. Whilst some people are born with silver spoons, this ancient primrose is more elusive. It was said to be the 'prima rosa' of each new flower year.

Betty possessed a kindred spirit with the wind. For all her life her front door was open. She loved people. This did not always please her husband, Bill, for forty years the estate mason. He liked to toast his toes, in the thick woollen socks she knitted for him, at a great fire of logs. He spent many icy days putting back everyone's slates that that wind had blown off. Battling with wind and other aspects of life made him a quiet, philosophical man.

Marjorie remembers her first garden. The family had moved into the courtyard, where just out of view, beside the joiners' shop, her father dressed his stone. And here in the evenings, he dressed and carved the gravestones.

Outside that fine open architectural space, great beech woods high and wild seemed to stretch in every direction. Not too far from the open back door, she found a space, perhaps a yard or two, under the trees, and grew her collection of double white primroses. Some neighbours had the double lilac, the old Quakers' Bonnet, but that was not common. Sir Charles's secretary, Edith Bulmer, knew this secret place and gave encouragement. This included a much treasured postcard sent from the Swiss Alps which showed a blue gentian. Edith B had a small cottage garden, and she knew about flowers.

Marjorie has always possessed the distinction of appreciating that the beauty of exceptional flowers is enhanced by a degree of isolation. Avid collectors who must always add something else, and more, ignore this. The magic in garden planting allows the prima donna to sing and permits the chorus to reply.

Meanwhile, I grew up at the edge of the Black Country. Clouds of men cycled by every morning, and cycled back after five o'clock. They worked in very small factories making nuts and bolts and locks. At a big holiday football match, as on Boxing Day, you could hardly find a path into the town's football ground. It was encircled by bicycles neatly parked at the edge of the pavements. But these would not need a lock, for no one would ever steal a man's bicycle.

I too had a small garden, but unlike the secret one at Wallington, made in woods with a deep rich covering of leaf mould, Midlands soil was sand and gravel. Apple trees were prolific but, unlike those in Worcestershire, were very small. I recall an early mission. I had spotted a shop selling pansies. A little cash, saved from my pocket money, was always to hand. Those colours were so rich, I had to have one, or was it two? My grandfather had taught me how to water when I planted his bedding plants, and he liked things done properly. Pansies were not much seen in local gardens and I cannot recall my success.

Marigolds and poppies were much better. Wild poppies were sometimes seen, but the Shirley ones were magnificent; marigolds had single flowers with orange or brown centres, and petals ranging from orange through yellow into the palest pastel cream.

Education was as different as environment. The northern two-roomed village school accommodated all local pupils, little girls and big boys alike, until they were fifteen. Later Marjorie came to know and like the schoolmistress well. Molly Thompson was well-read and well-travelled. She attended talks, political meetings, and the theatre and art galleries. In her neat village garden she grew madonna lilies and the Swiss blue gentian.

However, at the time, attending school was not as pleasing as it would have been to pursue the more serious businesses of life – exploring the woods and the river and climbing trees. She sometimes wondered whether Miss T would not have preferred to be walking in the woods too when the big boys were a little boisterous.

Then a wonderful opportunity occurred. When ten, she gained admission to a Saturday morning art class in the Fine Art department of the university. Applicants were welcomed with a serious talk by Quentin Bell, Vanessa's son and Virginia Woolf's nephew, who had grown up at Charleston, where he had been steeped in creativity. There was much competition.

In the huge still-life studio, full of students' easels supporting paintings of exotic plants and extraordinary objects, a picture must be made. The subject could be 'something from the past' or 'present hobbies'. In very thick and passionate paint, Marjorie produced her only known image of a dinosaur. This must have stood out clearly against well-rehearsed images of ponies and ballerinas. The class provided a marvellous escape into an alternative world. She discovered inner reserves of self-confidence and reliability.

Edith Bulmer allayed Betty's concerns, insisting that 'she must go,' and just before eight o'clock Marjorie joined the meandering country bus into the centre of Newcastle. After the class, she bought her lunch and waited until the bus reappeared at 2.15 to take everyone home. The News Theatre stood beside the bus station. After the Pathé cockerel called, a journey round the world began. In those black and white pre-television days this was good. Every two hours the show began again.

And then at thirteen, a further opportunity arose: she had the chance to leave the village, if she wished, and travel to a new large secondary school. The bus crossed the 'Wannie' hills to Bellingham, the last small market town before the road climbed away by Kielder into Scotland. It was a large new well-equipped thriving place. Marjorie and her best friend both loved it. When she was fifteen, the clear-sighted headmaster advised that, while she could stay and take GCEs, alternatively she could go directly to the City Art College.

Art school life was good – so many new subjects: lettering, typography, lithography, graphic design, display, illustration, drawing and painting. Staff had real experience of commercial life. Days were not long enough. And there were trips to see the London world. She stayed in youth hostels and walked and walked between the museums and the art galleries.

Each class in my school had over fifty pupils. It was a Victorian building with soaring, heavily-timbered ceilings and window sills so high that even a teacher might not be distracted by the world outside. It was surrounded by parks protected from us all by high iron railings. One had a bandstand and the other a fountain which was dramatically brought to life, spraying its ugly dolphins to celebrate the end of the war. I was very happy there.

Then I too was presented with an unexpected but wonderful means of independence. At eleven, I won a scholarship to the town's ancient grammar school. As a reward, my grandfather gave me a bicycle. It carried me and the watercolours ever further. My father may have helped. He was a devout socialist, and after the war, spent in a munitions factory, had refused a patronising offer of work in his in-laws' small factory. Instead, he found a job in a cycle factory in Birmingham: that was the source of my cycle.

Father took charge of great vats used in chromium plating. Although he loved literature, and amassed quite a library, he seems to have had leanings towards chemistry. His notebooks contained formulas and calculations. Every morning he left before six and returned just before eight in the evening. But he once spent a precious Saturday in taking me to see the factory. His colleagues seemed pleased to see his boy. The stench of those vats, which he constantly looked into, was inescapably vile. His lungs and back steadily collapsed until, though once athletic, he became permanently bent, creased like his old trilby. My mother resumed her profession, and took charge of an infants school in a poor part of town. She became the bread-winner.

I enjoyed the new school too until, when sixteen, a terrible decision had to be made. For the two years ahead, only three subjects could be followed, the groupings of which could not be altered. These were designed to lead you into your chosen profession. With no profession in mind, I chose classics. Then two less happy years later, with A-levels in Greek and Latin secured, I made an independent decision. I took an extra year and tried Art.

A week after my father's death, on a very cold Sunday in February, I boarded an extremely crowded train from Birmingham to Newcastle. My father had known that I was going. He had seen Newcastle in the First World War, and never forgot the beautiful Victorian garden, now a park, Jesmond Dene. Newcastle, of course, was full of snow. An icy bedroom had been booked for me in a small commercial travellers' hotel. On Monday I faced the entrance examination to the university's Fine Art department.

This was tucked into the corner of a quadrangle at the heart of a forest of buildings. You climbed a broad stone staircase past a magnificent weeping tree, and then opened a heavy door into a patterned, marble-floored entrance hall. Greeks and Romans were waiting, plaster casts among large potted plants.

Presently, I was in the still life studio where some years earlier Marjorie had painted her dinosaur. Here, like all my rivals, I must make a composition. I felt inexplicably elated, entirely free and liberated. My A-level course was leading me at its extreme point to Sickert, but now I took the thick wax crayons supplied and made my first abstract composition. I didn't know, but a surge into abstraction was the battle hymn of the times. I was admitted; my personal tutor was to be Quentin Bell.

Marjorie and I were art students in the same city, but attended different art schools. The university offered painting, sculpture and stained glass, while the art college offered diplomas in industrial, graphic, furniture and dress design. Each school had a potter, but nobody seemed to know why.

While Newcastle had many Chinese restaurants there was only one jazz club – and there was Marjorie! She was a wonderful dancer. But when all our various talents had been distributed, mine for rhythm and time, in a musical context, was entirely omitted. I was a sack of potatoes.

This was 1958. We were new people. We had a firm sense of belonging to the twentieth century. There was no reason to doubt that we would find something new for us to do. Yet we had no sense of what that might be.

Marjorie had discovered that she did not wish to find a commercial career in the design studios for which her newly acquired diploma had prepared her. It was time to get those GCEs. She was very talented, had great reserves of patience and determination but was not academic, yet she succeeded. I was not reassured by much kindly advice that a qualification in Fine Art would guarantee a safe and comfortable life in . . . teaching. Was there a connection? If you needed a sense of vocation, I had none.

We began our great adventure. In our long summer holidays, we set out to see our country. We had both particularly enjoyed the history of architecture which formed part of our A-level art syllabuses. Marjorie had taken English history at the same time. There were interesting connections. Plans and maps weren't necessary, with a base in the Midlands and another in Northumberland. We just needed to go; our extra-mural course began.

This was an astonishing time of free travel. Drivers in and after the war had been so happy to help soldiers on their precious journeys home. In our euphoric after-the-war times, their willingness to help blossomed to the benefit of anyone who raised their thumb at the roadside. It didn't matter that you were also carrying your tent, beds, food and clothes.

As a boy, I had been taken to see the great Midland castles and sometimes my grandfather took me to Moseley Old Hall, an Elizabethan house not far from home. For him, it was a working visit. He had experience in building so his eldest brother, Will, figurehead of their small stainless steel factory, 'the firm', sent him there, possibly to check work in hand. Great-Uncle Will was an antiquarian and his brothers had bought him this run-down place, which still continued to be used as a farmhouse. Will never moved out of his comfortable 'Jacobethan' detached, so close to his work, but had affection for this antiquity which had once provided a vital hiding place for young Charles II.

I had no idea of what actual business might be being transacted, but our reward was an invitation to return with family for a home-fed bacon tea. Bacon, still rationed, was a great treat. Even the small tins of bacon sent kindly by an Australian 'cousin' were still welcome after their long six-month sea voyage. (Australians who 'adopted' an English family and sent them food were called 'cousins' out of gratitude.) The housekeeper served us in a rather empty panelled room, perhaps at a gate-legged table on the uncarpeted floor of wonderful oak planks. After the cups of tea, cigarettes were lit and conversation began. My sister and I were then sent to the garden.

A path of blue Staffordshire brick, exactly as wide as the narrow back door, led into the garden. It was edged with well-kept yellow raspberries. But the garden had a strong smell, perhaps worse than the home-fed bacon. It had been claimed for the war effort. It was now home to the pigs. I loved that austere house. Its magical resources included secret hiding places, a priest-hole and an ancient painted chapel.

For Marjorie, Wallington had been such a marvellous place. Books from the library could be borrowed and should you walk into the central hall and find the Lady taking tea, she might ask you to join her. Everyone knew how the 'secret' mechanism of the huge lock on the huge back door worked.

Sir Charles occasionally took Marjorie with his secretary, Edith Bulmer, and son Martin to the People's Theatre in Newcastle where a robust company of amateurs regularly performed new and controversial plays. He had been a minister in the first socialist government. Politicians, theatre people and amateur painters were in the courtyard; miners' rallies were held and speeches made, and in the corner beside Marjorie's home, a youth hostel was made. Betty looked after the beds and kept the key. Everyone came to her open door for keys and directions.

We went to see the cathedrals. Near my home was Lichfield, of which we still have an inky drawing. Then came Coventry, Basil Spence's newly finished masterpiece. Architects appreciated painters; here were Graham Sutherland and John Piper. While outside the city was still much damaged, the cathedral seemed a wonderfully optimistic creation. Its cleanliness, sharpness and warm pink stone offered great hope. It seemed to take half a Sunday morning to reach Ely. We sat on a long bench upstairs in an oddly shaped bus, long and low and fat like the landscape, and saw its great mass miles away as we travelled through the oddest of landscapes, the Fens. It never seemed to get any nearer. Not far from Newcastle, we visited Durham; its massive arches sit on pillars deeply carved with the simplest and boldest geometric patterns which have such power and majesty.

We also looked into the small churches. There were Saxon windows in Bibury, Gloucestershire, and Bolam, Northumberland. We remain entranced by nearby Hartburn. At Escomb, in County Durham, which is unexpectedly encircled by possibly post-war council houses, a notice explained that we were in God's House. The ancient stone benches around the walls clearly offered hospitality. I had not heard this concept before. Outside the churches, their 'gardens' offered hollies and yews, sometimes beautifully clipped. Perfectly laid stone paths led back to finely designed gates and gateposts, and the gardens were surrounded by reassuring stone walls. These features, and stone benches too, are all now part of the structure of the garden at Hartington.

And then houses and then gardens. If you are to remake a house you need to understand its spaces, and those of gardens, too.

Great Dixter impressed on account of the completely improbable and hugely impressive work of its designer, Lutyens. The great border, perfectly proportioned, sits so happily beside the house Nathaniel Lloyd employed him to create. We possessed two of Nathaniel Lloyd's books. The topiary volume, *Garden Craftsmanship in Yew and Box*, records the early stages of his magnificent yew hedges and the stone paths he laid out. The peacocks were not so good then as they are now – one may even have lost its head – but personal experience since explains a lot – I would offer every sympathy! The other book, *A History of the English House*, has been a major source of inspiration and education. When we looked inside the house at Great Dixter, the furnishing was perfect and masterly.

On that same day we reached Sissinghurst; Marjorie was so happy that we had made that long journey. It was our only visit there, but the most impressive of all we made. It is the gold standard of gardens. We could not really claim to know it. Perhaps we stayed for three hours. Having lurked out of sight at 6 p.m., for a few extra moments it was briefly 'our garden'.

What magnificent design ordered those spaces, what nuances of colour and texture take you to its extremities, how brilliant the completely successful balancing of the huge white garden against the tiny cottage garden with flowers entirely in primary colours. You can speak of the art of gardening.

I wonder if 'Lawley's White,' the snow-white form of *Knautia arvensis* bought at Hartington by Sissinghurst's head gardener a few years ago for that white garden, still flourishes there. It is a vigorous northerner but it has charm.

Levens calls for superlatives too. The undreamt-of topiaries are so exquisitely maintained, and if you look down on to them from an upstairs window, you can see how expertly the garden was designed so long ago to fit it to the house. And you may think afterwards of how perfectly all those bedding plants serve that ever-rising garden of aristocrats above them.

But perhaps our greatest discovery was in Stratford-upon-Avon. It was not the river nor the theatre but the entrancing group of places belonging to the Shakespeare Trust.

Following signs through suburban edges of the town, dodging traffic, a long stretch of clipped hawthorn hedge, like a meeting of dinosaurs, confronted us. Along the pavement beside it, a crocodile of Japanese visitors was approaching this English shrine that is Anne Hathaway's cottage.

Inside the hedge, at right angles to it, set back behind a cottage garden, it was a monumental horizontal block, a perfect opposite to the Sissinghurst tower. Its organic straw roof was the likely inspiration for the shape of that hedge. Immediately to our left, inside the garden, a raised dais supported a very rustic arbour with a bench. This was the only space we had to ourselves. We had a privileged view of all, even a hint of the orchard beyond.

The garden planting was unsophisticated; here were the daisies, thrift and pinks we knew. The house border had clipped yews and ivy and the profuse white rose, *R. alba*. There was glorious furniture inside. A bed and a cradle from the family's remote past, and pieces of vernacular character, all looked so comfortably at home.

And three miles away another long old farm, Mary Arden's house, stood closely beside its lane. Just inside its low wall, warmly furnished with red valerian, there was just space for a very organic thin parterre. The box was well cut, but it had long forgotten any concept of horizontal top and matching vertical sides. It bulged and spread, denying any entry by path. An odd delphinium was trapped inside. The very narrow house border had topiarised shrubs, this time with clouds of the old pink and purple 'everlasting' sweet pea.

In the house the table stood a little in front of the inglenook fireplace. Here were the settle and the stool, and above them an encircling iron rail might once have carried a curtain. This might have held the last of the heat for a moment longer before you climbed up to a cold bedroom. You could have toasted toes here.

We had found very few small places like these. Unless the home of an inventor or creator of significance, they were not preserved to be looked at.

Instinctively feeling their value, we came to identify with these lesser places. Making small houses and gardens come to life seemed important. Could we thus contribute to our astonishing heritage? It was another reason for moving to Hartington.

Betty's kitchen at Wallington: a linocut of Marjorie stitching.

Marjorie busy with the sewing machine (1960).

A NEW PERSIAN MINIATURE   THE OIL CRISIS 1975

Marjorie's remarkably detailed drawing depicts Britannia (complete with waves) as distinctly oriental; only the land itself escapes, home to primrose, violet and daisy.

Marjorie tries a typewriter (1960).

Mother Evie in bed, after school.

Country vision and craftsmanship: 'Mr Tidy' of
Whittingham's garden.

Graham Thomas's parterre and pergola, Moseley Old Hall.

The White Garden and the Cottage Garden, Sissinghurst, as seen on our only visit.

Great Dixter: the wonderful response by a gardener to a very special house.

Levens Hall is a source of wonder: the gardener as sculptor.

Anne Hathaway's cottage: organic architecture with a real cottage garden.

Mary Arden's house with a very exuberant parterre.

CHAPTER THREE

THE ARTIST
AT WORK

By the time we moved into that little cottage at Wallington in 1964, we had both found employment at the College of Art. We had taken part-time teaching posts, and found a flat in a leafy suburb. Changing roles from student to lecturer implies that you know all the answers. The challenge was stimulating.

College terms were short, occupying barely half of the weeks of the year. The other half of time was ours; we could paint, travel or pursue hobbies if we had one. One colleague passionately wrote science fiction. We seemed to be well-paid but soon learned not to spend everything. Pay was calculated by the hours you worked. There were no retaining fees for holidays.

We drew and painted and enjoyed furnishing our little home. It was much more comfortable than the high, spacious Edwardian rooms we had occupied which were so cold. Yet, without noticing, we were drawn inescapably into the garden. We now see this period of our lives as our apprenticeship. As if we had just left school and had clear uncluttered minds, we wanted to learn everything. As in the art world, this meant doing everything. Herterton could not have been conceived without those thirteen years of toil and struggle.

After that first long warm summer, we awoke in the spring to a long thin rectangle of empty soil. Nothing relieved its emptiness. We felt the *horror vacui* which may confront the painter faced with his pristine, glowing new canvas, or the tribal weaver after he has inserted the first weft. All around us the community began to check the seed potatoes; the leek plants were in the frames. While harbouring no wish to disturb the peace, we felt the need to make a lawn.

Our enterprising Sunday newsagent now recommended *Amateur Gardening*. This was a new and fascinating experience. The editor was Arthur Hellyer, and contributors included Roy Hay, Percy Thrower and Margery Fish. These names became familiar. It was a pleasure to join Percy in his greenhouse, attending to the tomatoes. I have never wanted to own a greenhouse or to grow tomatoes, but this new community of experts made magic with seeds, plants and soil and their fingers.

How beautifully the grass grew in that renovated soil. We had followed the instructions well. But why did all those weeds grow too? Our project was much discussed, particularly in Betty's kitchen in the courtyard. Although no one had ever grown a lawn, advice was plentiful.

We knew that a lawn had neat edges beyond which it required a border. Familiar with the task of helping good causes through jumble sales, neighbours joined family in making contributions. You should never question motives behind gifts, but it is known that some plants are very nice and should be kept in the family, but possibly not in your garden . . .

It seemed good to have that wonderfully strong rudbeckia whose stout stems carry large brilliant yellow flowers which extend a sense of summer sunshine when the evenings have become short and the air feels thin and cold. But it could not be content with any simple space no matter how generous. Its thick searching roots spread in every direction as if to conquer the world. The old novae-angliae asters flower happily in October above vertical mountains of unrelieved greenery and perhaps explain a lot about the subsequent breeding of Michaelmas daisies. We received a red gladiolus and an old purple bearded iris which flowered for two weeks in June, a 'day-glow' red begonia and a spare plant of summer alyssum, a magenta polyanthus, a daisy, thrifts and pinks. Although the border may have been only three feet deep there were still lots of spaces.

Our neighbour Eddie, the head woodman, kept a deeply dug and heavily manured narrow strip below his large Victorian window. Here he provided the shock of summer. Out of his little greenhouse in June came trays of red begonias. These were counterpointed at the path edge by perfectly spaced plants of white alyssum and ultramarine lobelia. At the first whisper of imminent frost, however precocious, the precious tubers vanished, and the little border resumed its former state of emptiness.

Old Frank, our other neighbour, had worked all his life in the Wallington walled gardens. When we arrived, the last of his box edging lay upturned, drying and dying in the sun. It was too old-fashioned, and it harboured slugs. He knew a good plant, and could propagate by instinct. He had never thought of learning to drive and travelled to work on his old bicycle, but his lunchtimes were always long enough to carry out a small jug of water. The drops administered here and there kept everything in his little flower bed sparkling. When the National Trust took over the walled garden, he stepped down and modestly became the new head gardener's assistant. He had a nice smile for everyone, but never expressed opinions. As the new plants began to appear in the Wallington garden, it was a surprise to see what new treasures would appear in his plot. If you had to ask, you could always have a 'cutting'.

We knew that gardening was just a hobby. It was very enjoyable. But questions arose. Just what were we doing? Why did you need a lawn with a narrow border?

Help now came from a new Tuesday afternoon caller. Once a fortnight, the travelling library van arrived. This became a special delight. The lady in charge said she could locate and bring any book not in the van should we wish to read it. We found, indeed, that no reference library, whether in a university or a great city centre such as Glasgow, was immune from her efforts. Sometimes she confided that what she had brought for us was already a month overdue for return. 'Just keep it now, but I must have it back in four weeks.'

Were there any garden history books? Eventually, *A History of Gardening in England*, the pioneering work of Alicia Amherst from the 1890s, arrived, then *The Story of the Garden* by Eleanour Sinclair

Rohde, some of whose other books also introduced us to herbs and herbals, and then Ralph Dutton's succinct account, simply called *The English Garden*. Gardens had not always been a matter of neat lawns and narrow borders.

Everyone knew that Capability Brown had attended the village school. Surviving relatives still lived near his birthplace. Eddie's friend, Cecil Brown, had given us a plant; he was a local master leek grower. His predecessor had walked this unique landscape, seen its contours and curving rivers. Some said that he had recreated Northumberland all over the rest of England. It looked as if his passion for green spaces had passed down into all our suburban spaces. Perhaps grass is good for us?

Eddie introduced us to an old friend who had been a lifetime market gardener who also grew and sold plants. His passion was for alpine gardening, and he sent us to see the Edinburgh Botanical Gardens. We visited several times every year and made notes. And now we began to spend afternoons in the walled garden at Wallington, making notes there. As the new planting progressed, a forest of labels sprang up. In the evenings we could look up the plants in our new purchase: Roy Hay's updated edition of William Robinson's *The English Flower Garden*.

We recognised that gardens needed protective boundaries. Important ones had walls; our cottage garden would have hedges. Our choices were not good. For one side we had beech. In winter the leaves are still there, rattling and brown, but the late spring growth pushes them off to lodge in all your plants where they do not quietly go away. For the other we had lonicera. This will enslave you as surely as privet. For the end of the lawn, rugosa roses. They had large hips in the autumn. They will both invade and prickle you. Purely by chance, we found some edging box too (*Buxus suffruticosa*). In a quiet local lane where the verge widened lay several short lengths of edging recently uprooted and ruthlessly deposited. Marjorie soon propagated enough for a small hedge.

Most of all it seemed that gardens required quantities of distinguished plants. We had to extend our expeditions beyond architecture and gardens to include nursery gardens. Not many had survived the war and new ones seemed mainly concerned to meet the feverish demand for roses, the new floribundas and hybrid teas. The blacksmith's wife smiled with delight. At last she had persuaded 'him' to dig out all their remaining herbaceous plants. She had ordered two dozen mixed roses from Aberdeen.

Amateur Gardening carried small adverts from nurserymen, though then the pages were mainly filled by articles and a few black and white photos. The Sunday papers had increasingly popular commentators whose pages were filled at the edges with small adverts too. Marjorie was very good at spotting the places we needed to find. There were not many and they were well scattered. We still have a few of their early catalogues or lists which were sent to you on request. Much the most important find was Margery Fish, who had already charmed us by her magazine articles.

Her book, *Cottage Garden Flowers*, described field trips into local villages, searching for good plants. Sensitive old gardeners like our neighbour Frank must have taken a few favourites home when, perhaps with some regret, the pre-war flower borders in the walled gardens had to be removed. The treasures were not confined to the rural cottages; they might equally be seen growing in front of small neat terraced houses in the city, or even under hedges. Plants travelled and became heirlooms. It was better than hunting in the Andes or the Himalayas, which had claimed so many brave lives. We followed her example.

She closed her garden in July, though her nursery and its staff were still available. That afforded the chance to take her busman's holiday and do her chosen visits. But you could still visit her on Saturday mornings by appointment when at home in her private July time.

Before compiling our list, there was much preparation to be done. We have three of her catalogues. A few sheets of neatly typewritten paper perhaps six inches square carried Latin names, without further explanation, in alphabetical order. One of our copies still carries Marjorie's neat annotations. Between each line she researched and provided an English interpretation. What were prunellas? Of course we knew the carpets of tiny wild ones in the Wallington woods, but they were 'self-heals'. . .

We found a farm quite close to East Lambrook where we could set up our tent and arrived at the Manor exactly on time. She was a quiet, attentive and serious lady. She gave me her large barrow, took up her fork and, with no ceremony, the morning's work began. Our list was prepared and modest. She lifted small pieces for us from her borders, sometimes muttering, 'Ah, yes . . .' But sometimes she asked if we knew this other form of the plant just slipped into the barrow, or its relative, just over there? We were quite beguiled and, after two hours, the barrow was really full. There were not only the relatives of the plants we had requested, and their other forms or colours, but some of the unknown treasures from in between. She could have continued, it was our heads that were swimming. She loved plants and she liked people who liked her plants, and she liked people to have her plants. She was never jealous or guarded.

Then we were in the old Malthouse for the wrapping. It was such a shock when the plants were lifted out on to the bench; for she deftly removed any trace of her precious soil (she was very wise). We noticed a large heap of moss, and she took small pieces which she wrapped around the roots, dipped the plant into her large wooden rainwater barrel just outside by the doorway, added a small piece of ready-torn newspaper, a neatly written label and an elastic band. 'Would we now like to step indoors with her while she prepared our invoice?' We modestly declined. We had taken up a lot of her time. Her prices were not high; 'ordinary' plants cost one shilling and sixpence (7p), specials two and six (12p) and, should you be tempted, the rarest of rarities would cost you three and six (almost 18p).

We would have always liked more time in that garden. Marjorie found it somewhat unkempt. It was not planted for show. It was rather like an endless collection of 'cabinets of curiosity'. You would only discover what was there if you looked deeply and carefully. She knew exactly what was where, but you would never have been able to guess. She was in charge of the garden; the nursery staff lived in the nursery. She may have supplied them with stock, but she was the gardener and her assistant was her hairdresser's son, and he was just fifteen! We visited her three times before she died at eighty-five in 1969.

Our acquisitions were eventually shared with Wallington's new head gardener. He was Northumbrian but was 'imported' from the Manchester Botanic Garden. He was related to Mr Keith, a well-respected head gardener in earlier times who had written three books about Wallington and a novel. If you knew where he had lived, you would notice different plants in the verges nearby. The wood anemones had double flowers, the cranesbills were quite different, and you might even find a 'Jack in the Green' primrose. We made beneficial exchanges and were occasionally invited to supper in his comfortable courtyard cottage. His life was ever devoted to 'his' walled garden and, like old Frank, his views were not shared with the neighbours.

The National Trust agent had 'windows' into the community. I don't know whether he knew that we knew! In 1968 he brought us a visitor whose opinions on our progress he would value: Graham Thomas. His modest manner and measured speech – his remarks were always both precise and constructive – encouraged us to explain all our ideas of both design and plants. He was sympathetic.

When he had joined the Trust as the first Gardens Advisor it was a part-time post, for they then only possessed seven gardens. Like Margery Fish, he too was engaged in the great 'British Plant Hunt', but his target was the recovery of the old shrub roses. They had been sacrificed from the large gardens with the herbaceous material. Now, he was much busier but still spent two separate weeks a year at Wallington. He visited us on Friday afternoons before beginning his long journey back to Surrey. A cup of tea and a good slice of fruitcake we hope made it more comfortable.

Once he puzzlingly said that 'It takes twenty years to make a garden, and you should make two, perhaps three.' After less than ten years, having made many fresh starts, alterations and replantings, we knew that things were not quite finished, but could it really take that long? Now, as we come close to forty years' work at Herterton, we have a better understanding of time. We still have things to do.

We never discussed his local work, but on one occasion he related an incident. On one afternoon during his week, he reported his plans to the local voluntary National Trust Committee. Their cars were permitted in the courtyard so that everyone knew what was going on! There was then no permanent member of staff appointed as historic buildings advisor, and a prominent local lady with great enthusiasm, flair and talent had taken on that role on a voluntary basis. She was vociferous and opinionated, and in her own large walled garden she grew the 'very best' collection of old shrub roses, with over two hundred varieties. Perhaps to impress Graham and everyone else present, she announced that she had just taken a holiday in Persia where she had visited the Shah's garden. This was then an undreamt-of luxury. His response was calm and considered. 'Ah, yes,' he said, 'I designed it for him.' We thought we noticed a slight curve in his lip as if he had nearly permitted himself to smile. I have since imagined that the lady's great Daimler, which always headed the line of cars, may have driven away quietly that afternoon.

His work at Wallington engrossed us. Inside the gate a long border ran towards the conservatory, topped by its gazebo. This had formerly been the cut-flower bed. Lady Trevelyan cycled down to the garden on Friday morning and selected some flowers for the house; after lunch Frank cycled back to deliver them. In the afternoon she could arrange them for the weekend's visitors to see. Below a terrace to the right, Bill had made Molly's Folly (Molly was Lady T) before the war; water trickled into a small pool, set within a distinctive curling wall which swept down to enclose the surrounding paving. After that, there had been fruit and vegetables, then clusters of greenhouses for the tomatoes. Marjorie had spent her student summers working with old Frank, picking raspberries and gooseberries to his orders.

Now this part was landscaped, and her father, Bill, created a curving rill, edged with stones and alpine plants. On the left side a long alpine wall, to the right a deep shrub border with collections of ground cover plants, a new concept. (Both Margery Fish and Graham wrote, very differently, books on ground cover.) In front of the conservatory a brilliant display of bedding plants appeared, then a blue and yellow walk, overarched with climbers on iron supports. It sloped down to a large roundel which Bill laid out in the very best stone slabs, and this was surrounded by yew hedging. A large central area, enclosed by old yew hedges, was cleared of vegetables and became an arboretum. Neat lines of trees with high clean trunks were planted perfectly and evenly spaced over turf. Here you could study variations upon several favourite small tree families such as hawthorns and crabs. You might notice their evolving shape, their bark, their leaf colours and shapes, then flowers and fruits. It was a refreshing surprise after the low alpines, the lawns and the lumpy masses of shrubs. And in the lowest section, where the garden walls continued to step down so beautifully and dramatically as the land fell towards the great iron gates, now quite close to the river, grass returned. The jumble of old greenhouses was removed and water reappeared in a new small lake which complemented the two eighteenth-century ones you had already passed on your walk through the woods towards the walled garden. But the first old cut-flower bed was itself a remarkable conception.

Climbers and some shrubs reached up and beyond the twelve-foot-high wall. There were enormous shrubs, grasses and foliage plants with perennials and biennials and front edges with violas and prostrate artemesias. It was wonderfully orchestrated, in the same way as the great border at Great Dixter, and as the only image we knew (a watercolour by Helen Allingham in an old book we possessed, *Happy England*, by Marcus Huish) which showed the great border Gertrude Jekyll had created at Munstead. G.J. loved colour and her great tapestry, backed by tree foliage, as at Wallington, glowed warmly. However, the colour Graham had chosen to celebrate was grey.

When visiting my mother, we went to see his work at Moseley Old Hall which proceeded simultaneously. Uncle Will had died in 1959 and his widow gave it to the Trust. There was a problem with the endowment, but the good people of Wolverhampton made great efforts to raise what was required. Graham explained his process. A year was spent in researching the gardening books of the Elizabethan age, and a search was made to find and identify flowers named in the works of Shakespeare. The much photographed parterre was created, and a long pergola of the finest intricate joiner work was added. In the small garden space at the front of the house, a lawn with small flower beds was edged along the path with yew pyramids. In the sparse flower beds we saw for the first time 'Fair Maids of France' (*Ranunculus aconitifolius* 'Flore Pleno'), the blue *Teucrium fruticans* and, so nice to see, the field cornflower which was not generally to be seen in serious gardens then. Graham, of course, sent us the 'Fair Maids'.

If ever a plant was mentioned to him, when all our known sources failed, he took a tiny notebook out of an inner pocket; without fail the plant arrived in November, sometimes directly from one of 'his' important gardens.

At Sissinghurst we saw the art of gardening, and now we realised that we had actually seen the artist at work.

Our little garden gradually acquired form. We came to understand the importance of strategy. You needed clearly defined sections with separate policies, and you should not repeat any planting. Each plant should have its role to play.

The upper part, at the front door, became a cottage garden and this had the greatest concentration of flowers. By 1975, when our collection of plants grown in that quarter of an acre numbered more than two thousand different items, our beautiful lawn had shrunk to a curving path less than three feet wide. At its centre within the gentle curves was a small collection of shrub roses. To house the last one we had to, willingly, demolish the raised alpine bed we had made from blocks of peat cut locally. That was an odd reminder of a brief passion for alpines engendered by Eddie's old nurseryman friend. Then you passed to a second section, initially our fruit and vegetable garden. Here we made a new lawn, edged in box. The box enclosed a pair of beds devoted to shrubs, with ground cover plants. A grey-leaved willow was paired with the purple- and blue-flowered sibirica irises. But what a lot you had to think of. Its orange bark glowed in the winter sun, but at iris time it was hidden by the grey leaves. These looked good with the irises, but the exciting confrontation of the complementary colours of orange and blue which we had devised just could not work. And the final, smallest part, at the bottom of the garden, below an overhead canopy of leaves from the limes and beeches at the edge of the wood, was home to 'shady' plants. We had had to remove a thirty-foot spread of dogwood which had happily leapt over the low stone boundary wall. We made a small collection of appropriate plants. *Plants for Shade* was another of Margery Fish's books, and her famous ditch garden was in shade. Primulas became of interest, but the giant Tibetan 'cowslip', *Primula florindae*, so proud and happy at Wallington, was soon reduced to less than the size of an English cowslip. The great trees' roots had long ago claimed all our soil down there for their nourishment.

Our way of life was checked in 1970. After a year or more of negotiations, strictly by full-time staff, the Art College merged with the two other major further education colleges in the city, technology and commerce, to form the new Newcastle Polytechnic. These other colleges had small non-specialised art staffs, and all had to be accommodated under this new roof. There could be no more part-timers, at least for a while. We were offered full-time posts, a career at last. It would mean holiday pay, a safe position, with promotions and pensions in prospect.

It would also mean no more long holidays. The regular staff held interminable planning and policy meetings which continued long after we and the students had left, and which resumed long before new ones arrived and courses began.

It was not difficult to choose the alternative, which meant an isolated, independent journey into gardening. The beauty of freedom was the beauty of life. All temptations on offer had to be refused.

In 1966 we had made a small nursery bed from which plants could be lifted for sale. It was beside a path at the edge of our raspberries. Sir Charles's youngest daughter, Patricia, occupied an upstairs flat in 'The Hall', as we always called the mansion. She possessed all the great Trevelyan energy and enthusiasm. She leased a corner of the courtyard from the Trust where she created a café and invented a shop. All items in the shop were to be locally homemade. She came to see us. What could we make for her: pottery, pictures, knitting? Bill, who had just retired, made himself a greenhouse to grow all the tomatoes, cucumbers and lettuces which would be required. His allotment also produced cut flowers, daffodils and tulips in the spring and chrysanthemums in the autumn, and since he kept thirty-three hives of bees, he made a lot of honey. All sold well. We had no time to produce any of the items Patricia suggested, but within a day Marjorie thought of plants. Even in 1966 our plants could not be allowed to get very large; our spaces were rapidly filling up. We were already composting good surplus things. We were supplied with a large baker's tray, and this was returned quite quickly with our first tiny plants wrapped in newspaper. I walked through the woods three days later to see what had happened. Everything had disappeared. We had fixed our prices in deference to Margery Fish. We had only two rates, one and threepence (6p) and two and threepence (11p). The expensive ones had a black patch at the top corner of their labels. Patricia was not greedy; she was pleased to have them, and took a modest token.

That autumn I called at an accountant's. It was a little upstairs room close to Woolworths in our former leafy suburb's High Street. I had never met such a person before and found him friendly if a little surprised. 'Is that all? Think no more about it, but if you feel in two or three years' time that it might take off, come back and see me.' Our nursery was three feet deep and fifteen feet wide.

In 1970, it was essential to expand. After negotiations for the extra piece of land were completed, Tom, Betty's neighbour, the Trevelyan's old ploughman, brought his tractor and ploughed it for us. Eddie fenced it stoutly. We dug it and laid out the 'working beds' and a stock border along its length. We preserved the fifteen foot length of the nursery bed in the garden and made each bed an exact width which allowed you to reach its centre from either side so that you never had to stand on the soil. There may have been ten beds. On account of the oak tree the ground was L-shaped, and in the short leg there was space for our gooseberries, raspberries, currants and some herbs, edged with two old polyanthus, a gift from Frank. When a year later we had a plant list, Graham added us to his special list of suppliers which went annually to National Trust head gardeners. Some plants went to good places.

Marjorie deployed her plants directly into rows of about twelve. The straight lines were created by the light imprint of the rake's long handle, and inserted from both sides of the bed. The intervening paths were two feet wide. The design proved functional, and still serves us at Hartington. And now, as then, everything lifted is wrapped in newspaper. This can be disposed of in several ways, much more satisfactorily than black polythene.

The selling season at best is only six months long, although the garden work lasts for at least twelve. It was always necessary for me to find various other temporary winter employments for us to survive.

In 1971 my uncle, Maurice Wiggin, gave the nursery its first publicity. He wrote for many years for the *Sunday Times* and had just 'nearly' retired. He had moved into a cottage in Worcestershire, his wife's county. It was close to his beloved River Teme, for he was a passionate angler. (*The Passionate Angler* was the title of one of his books.) His retirement meant that he just did regular book reviews, and wrote a weekly 'country' column.

Since he had always been kind to us, often sending us thoughtful books, Marjorie thought of sending him a parcel of her new nursery plants as a housewarming present. All had good old English names – 'purple gromwell,' 'blue-eyed Mary' and even a piece of white 'blue-eyed Mary' that we had been astonished to spot growing under a washing line in a rather isolated hamlet not far from Wallington – and there were perhaps a dozen altogether. Soon we had a phone call and, oddly, a request to check exact details of our address. When on Sunday we opened our paper to see his column, we found that it was all about old country plants, English plant names, and our nursery. By the following weekend we had received over a hundred requests for a plant list. Some were written on Houses of Parliament notepaper. And Marjorie had created a plant list of 150 plants, all with English as well as Latin names, and I had devised our plant labels. Our little business had begun.

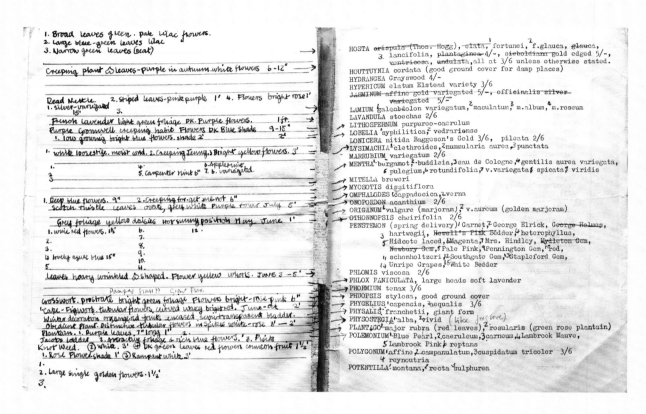

A page in a Margery Fish catalogue annotated by Marjorie in preparation for our visit.

Marjorie's record book (1967) with Margery Fish labels carefully glued down.

Above left: the cottage in 1964.
Above right: the cottage garden in 1975.
Opposite: 'Molly's Folly' in the Wallington walled garden with the
new Graham Thomas stream and rockery in the foreground (*c.* 1970).
Following page: *Geum* 'Herterton Primrose'.

Part Two

TAKING STOCK

CULTURALLY REFRESHED

Matisse said that nothing grows in the shade of a great tree. He disbanded the small circle of followers who had come, as pilgrims, to work in his company. Ralph Vaughan Williams had worked with Ravel, but he did not become Ravel; yet Matthew Smith, who worked beside Matisse, probably would not have become Matthew Smith if he had not done so. In the twentieth century, having followers might seem irksome to the master, and being a follower might not benefit the acolyte.

Of course, Matisse was a great painter. Taken literally his statement could be contested by a gardener. Vita Sackville-West would have devised instant strategies for such a predicament, and the owner of the humblest space overhung with no matter whose tree may contrive to grow an unimaginable range of plants in unimaginable containers if the finger of garden magic should touch them. Taste is an unaccountable factor.

After thirteen years of living at Wallington, we were now moving away from that great tree and the shade and the spell it cast over our lives. But we had been so lucky. We had actually been 'in the right place at the right time'. That is everyone's dream whether you play football or politics. In the later 1960s we had witnessed the moving of dynasties. Sir Charles had envisaged this in 1941; he had died in 1958, his wife in 1966, and then it was time for the National Trust.

In the early 1970s, the Trust must have felt proud of the work it had already done at Wallington, since it published a special booklet about it. This contained five major articles which had appeared in *Country Life* between April 1970 and May 1971. John Cornforth wrote about the house, Michael Archer about the ceramic collection, and Arthur Hellyer about the garden. The photographs recorded brilliant achievements. They demonstrated that Wallington was a centre of high culture. Art had been commissioned there and happily that tradition was to continue.

Lady Pauline, whose sketchbooks are still in the library, had entertained a wide circle of painters and poets in the 1850s. The central hall was created then, and frescoes and floral decorations were added. John Ruskin was a contributor. It is no surprise that the art of gardening has always flourished here. It is said that in the late summer of 1976 when all greenery had reached the outer edge of survival, the outlines of an ancient parterre appeared in ghostly manner in the fine turf of the west lawn, beside the house. Gardening belongs quite properly to civilised places.

In 1962, you could enjoy a leisurely walk through what survived of the eighteenth-century landscaping, to see the marvellous Edwardian conservatory in the walled garden. After our wedding in the village on a sunny Saturday in August, the remaining members of the small group of close relatives who had shared lunch in Betty's cottage, but had not visited Wallington before, joined in a stroll to see the brilliant show of fuschias and pelargoniums and to sniff the scents of vanilla and lemon. On that happy day, all the purest joys and bounties of the world were ours to share for a moment.

After 1964, those mesmerising green beech woods became a place of study. There were so many unknown plants under the towering trees. Asarabacca (*Asarum europaeum*) took a long time to identify. Even the modest flowers of dog's mercury were always something to look forward to in February. However cold it was, at last something was stirring.

The perfectly sited half-circular Chippendale seat, then probably held together in some places by generous coats of George's paint – George was the last estate painter – demanded that you sit in the centre if only for a moment to look down on the China pond and its old low boathouse. Was there a boat there, and did the pond really show the shape of China? The seat always seemed to have been placed in an outdoor green cathedral with silvery arching pillars of beech. It sat on a carpet of moss.

Then there were the walls. The path through the wood broadened and straightened into a highway. A wall twelve feet high appeared on your left with, at its centre, the 'Portico'. The classical stone pediment sits on stone pillars and encloses a modest stone-paved space. At the back was a simple green door with a square light above. In front, a 1740 green-painted Windsor chair and an octagonal 'Gothick' table with a marble top were carefully placed.

Behind the green door was a very small cottage. Marjorie recalls Mrs Wright's old sofa. For this, during the war, she had knitted a unique cover of string. The very long path behind the high wall to her back door passed through many wild flowers including a species of scilla we have not yet identified. Opposite the front door was a surprise. The trees parted and revealed a dramatic bright walk down to the Garden pond. It preserved the width of the portico, and the sun lit the mown grass. The view from the far side of the pond, edged with rushes and lush wild vegetation, back up the grassy slope through the dark wood to the Grecian portico enclosing its perfect composition of chair, door and table, was spectacular and theatrical. The great wall seemed to be a part of a stage set conceived on a heroic scale.

The wall was said to be the labour of village folk who set to and made those hundreds and thousands of bricks from their local clay. Then twenty years later, in 1760, they must have started again when the 'new' enclosed walled garden of four and a half acres was built at the end of the pond a little further down the slope to the river. Those walls were a monumental labour commissioned for the sake of art. They also made a crucial contribution to the landscape, their colour a wonderful contrast to the natural elements outside which they deny, and to the plants inside which they succour. Brick was a rare, aesthetically valued element in eighteenth-century Northumberland, where stone was the universal building material employed.

Lady Pauline's sketchbook diaries note a portico wall disaster. After a venerable life and a major battle against a vicious autumnal gale, valiant old '?' (all 'important' old trees were given Christian names, now forgotten, and somehow this one suggested that of an admiral lost in service) fell, and went down through the wall. Poor old '?'; after all, walls can be rebuilt.

In that wood, you would pause at odd mounds of collected stones. These included double-sided heads, other fragments of bodies, shields, swords, and just over the road, four large toothy dragon heads defend the house, set well back behind a majestic lawn. It is said that architectural fragments perhaps from London city walls and gates travelled back to Newcastle in the empty coal boats. They were sold at the quayside to eager town and country gentlemen to add cultural depth to their estates. These distributed monumental fragments from the past certainly added a sense of mystery to the garden and sounded the humbling message that all we create will decay and fall. In gardens, only the gardeners' daily efforts will preserve the achievement for just one more day.

The great house was so important too. We could attend the Lady's tenants' Christmas party. This was not a bacchanalian feast since the Trevelyans were 'teetotal'. Indeed, it was not a feast at all for there were no refreshments. But for a couple of hours on a black December night, you shared the house with the Lady. Inside was warm and bright. You hung up your coat, and walked, and sat and talked. Just to 'see and be seen' was a satisfying occupation for local folk 'at the times of all gatherings'. It was not yet the time of motor cars. All who attended, except for a few of the 'out by' farming tenants, came on foot. Everyone was smart, everyone was excited. Some explored the many photo albums, for Lady T liked to have a record of everyone with their families, and there were books of Trevelyan photos, and the diaries and sketchbooks. Just before nine everyone gathered in the central hall for the Lady's message of good wishes, and notes of recent happenings. Then, coats on, through that great back door, under the huge lantern, quick footsteps led into the black night. You may be going home to make your supper, but you felt culturally refreshed.

Lady Mary, who was known to her intimate family as Molly, had kindly given Betty some fragments of William Morris wallpaper. While at art college Marjorie had made these into a collage which recreated the pattern. For this design, Morris had chosen campions, meadow fritillaries and field cornflowers, all beautifully drawn. The fragments had come to hand when the 'old rain' got in again and Bill was sent up to the roof. It seemed to be possible with neat fingers to tear damp paper back to an agreeable line just a little further below the ceiling, and then all looked well again. She also brought Betty a fragment of Morris's woven material in the dragon and pheasant design. Perhaps with the pressure of generations of large families the old sofa's cover just fell to pieces. For Lady T, Marjorie sometimes carried a parcel of textile fragments to one of the last surviving early Victorian furnishing shops in Newcastle, where, once the contents had been cleaned, repairs would be carried out. Now the collage colours have faded into pale medieval blues, pinks and nearly greens which Morris would probably have appreciated; the woven fragment made a perfect cushion for Marjorie's dolly (made for her by Betty), who still always looks so cheerful in her cradle.

The National Trust called the great John Fowler to the house. When it came to hanging pictures, it meant Saturday work for Bill and George. 'Up a little, and a little to the left . . . Hold . . .' I came to know about 'holding' when Bill built his greenhouse. Those clean and innocent lengths of timber always had to be held at least at arm's length above your head and kept still and . . . 'Up.' The nails were then driven in from above, 'against' your 'unfailing' strength. But there would be cake and honey for tea.

An invasion of Scottish painters had followed and they stayed for an entire winter. There was so much new paint to put on. It was said that no fewer than eight shades of that elusive pale, grey-blue were used on the doors and architectural details of the great central saloon. People had to come to see if they could identify and spot them. It was perfectly painted, and when all was finished the house possessed a noble simplicity and clarity. Any dull Victorian colours and clutter had been swept away.

Lady T had fed her dog from Ming bowls. That had ceased. The magnificent ceramic collection, said to be second in significance to only one other, was beautifully assembled. For the cabinet interiors, John Fowler devised a superbly subtle dark, warm grey. Whites, blues and occasional colours glowed. Corridors and passages had clean light stone floors and walls of perfectly hung and labelled paintings. You might be standing in a Dutch interior. The carpets, all of which were perfect sizes for the great rooms and some of which were now dated to the early nineteenth century, looked as remarkable as they were.

The green library had tall cases of leathered books, old red chairs, a red tiled fireplace, all supported by the glowing reds and blues of the early Ushak carpet in a very rare design. The great saloon was an exquisite Whistler study of grey-blues and gold resting on a glorious sea of soft green and turquoise to be seen only in the best of antique Fereghan carpets. In the dining room, the long table with red seated chairs stood on the best soft red and light blues of a very early Turkey carpet in front of more and more rare ceramics, against pale grey walls. The Lady's parlour had paper and a carpet from William Morris.

From the front door you walked into a smaller entrance room. Here the Ziegler Fereghan carpet had an exceptionally broad warm brown border which seemed to hint that there might be an element of Vandyke Brown in John Fowler's ever mysterious not quite grey in the cabinets. At the leathered desk a comfortable country lady sat in a warm knitted cardigan. Her round pink face was tanned, she wore large glasses, had a Homeric nose and a large smile. She was Marjorie's mother, Betty. Lady T trained her as her first house guide just before the war and she had been a very attentive student. She took the entrance fees.

People came to see the huge collection of dolls' houses, all perfectly furnished and equipped. Some came because of the important needlework, all homemade, which the late Margaret Swain had written about in *Country Life*. The American author Joan Edwards in her *Crewel Work in England* described Lady Mary's own contribution as the finest piece of English crewel work of the twentieth century. Her 'tapestry' as everyone locally described it, had taken twenty-three years of absolute devotion to complete. It was a great achievement. The book reproduced a watercolour of her diligently at work. Military people were interested in the huge collection of lead soldiers. Trevelyans who knew and wrote history studied the tactics employed in great British battles. They had huge resources of 'troops' to manoeuvre. Geological specimens and early toys were in the house museum.

In Betty's courtyard cottage there were innumerable gatherings of workers, neighbours and travellers in the small kitchen. It was sufficiently far from the open back door to feel warm and cosy. There were amazing discussions and revelations. If the local newspaper arrived late it was dismissed as 'history'. News travelled on the wind, and it passed through that tiny room from dawn to dusk. When many years later Betty died, almost ninety-four, destroyed by many years of malicious and unrelenting Alzheimer's, we emptied her final cottage and returned her key. We came upon her collection of diaries. Every night she made her record. But there were no revelations. It was instantly clear that she never deviated from her two priorities; she remembered first the weather and second the egg yield.

At midday men came to eat their sandwiches, their 'bait', with Bill. They talked of weather, gardens and bees. Bill found it absurdly funny when one bee man related that he had been faced with a sudden swarm. He had no option but reached for his airgun and shot the queen in flight, one among so many.

In the early evening ladies returning from the hen field called in with Betty. Mrs Masson, the old Scottish lady, was very shy but in that intimate place she would confide, 'Oh, I dee like a garden . . . but I deena like to work in a garden.' The Massons had an allotment opposite the old wooden barn just past Betty's door. Now in their eighties, they made separate visits several times a day. Bob worked, Marion picked the fruit, and she knew exactly what Bob had done. The garden was kept in perfect order and had two vegetable plots edged with fruit bushes and flowers, all surrounded by narrow flower borders. Bob had been a head forester and they had lived in various places including Herefordshire. He still went away in his vintage Rover to do a little extra gardening for clients from whom he had acquired some interesting plants. He had found *Gladiolus illyricus*, and it must be said that 'Creeping Jenny' (*Lysimachia nummularia*) has never looked better than when grown in generous carpets under his ripening gold-green gooseberries.

A prized traveller came from the woollen mill ten miles away in Betty's home village. He carried lengths of fine cloths for skirts, coats and jackets, and samples of the thick woollen blankets, plaids and 'rugs' often laid over the backs of chairs and sofas. Small samples could be made into double-sided patchwork blankets which were extra warm on the coldest nights. Some said that the best brushes and shovels came down with the man from Jedburgh. His suitcases carried treasures now difficult to match.

The table was always in use. On baking day, the week's supply of cakes, biscuits, scones and toffee was made. At night, it was for dressmaking, mat-making and sewing. Jams and marmalade were made, or it could be home to the extractor and jars of honey, and for the honey sections that had to be carefully scraped before they could be delivered.

I noticed that in many conversations 'common sense' was mentioned. I didn't recall hearing of this in the Midlands, perhaps it was something we lacked? It was much praised, and anyone's actions which demonstrated a lack of this quality were scorned and regretted. Expressed through the hands of the craftsmen we were to employ in the years of construction work ahead at Hartington, it became a life-enhancing joy. And when garrulous Betty had to deal with the inquisitive and curious ones, who sought her opinions of her unusual daughter and her not even northerner son-in-law, she would quell their curiosity by explaining, 'Well, you see, they have a different religion from us.' That was more than some could ever bear to know. In spite of what Bill and even her daughter may have sometimes said, she possessed common sense too. She kept faith in us.

And what was sometimes said of us? 'They go to university and then what do they do? Just scrattin' aboot in the groun', like bairns.' It was a disgrace. The Hartington experience ahead was to entail three years of intensive soil work for which 'scrattin'' would have been a hugely inadequate term.

After our many years of art school life, the Wallington experience had been so rich, so busy, so diverse. We had benefited from the open-door culture of the end of the Trevelyan era, and from access to the end of the undisturbed village culture and close observation of the splendid new work of the National Trust. We had known the jumble sales distinguished by the donations from Wallington attics and wardrobes. The wealthier folk who rented Trevelyan houses – Sir Charles had left property to all of his children – added their support too. Every late spring at 'term-time', when once folk moved from farm or cottage, the mart doors opened to receive the unwanted furniture and heirlooms, the clocks, the exotic teapots and cheese dishes, the garden tools, the hand tools, the winter's spare homemade rugs, the turnip skeps . . . Everyone looked forward to the following great early summer clearance sale, a real 'see and be seen' event. Great treasure could be bought for threepence (1½p), a clock for sixpence (2½p). And in the village hall there might be a Christmas concert where visiting Trevelyans could perform astonishing recitals. We had met craftsmen who did everything for everyone, even repairing your old television set. And should you require any other skill, someone would be acquainted with just the right person.

We had felt the pulse of that busy life. Being busy was also the culture of the painter, that artist who has always more to do. 'You must make your work your pleasure,' was Bill's advice. He was a happy man who loved to work.

We had met so many people who had so variously expressed their love of gardening. So many plants had been collected. There were families of hostas, irises, euphorbias, primulas, alpines, herbs . . . Indoors we had collected furniture and carpets. We had found our way to the salerooms and had discovered the dealers. We had found that gardening had fitted into our culture and had accepted the calling to that community.

We did not feel that we had sacrificed our creative independence to the great 'tree' of Wallington, and there were no regrets when the removal van set off on the three-mile journey. We felt well prepared for our new life. It seemed as if we had received a really first-class English breakfast.

Had Matisse feared for his own integrity or for that of his pupils? Or did he realise in 1912 that he had no time for teaching; he had far too much work to do?

The ancient gargoyles which protect Wallington House.

Above: Tom the ploughman's barn and the clock-tower. Betty's cottage is just visible between the barn's second and third timber pillars.
Opposite: Marjorie's drawing of Betty's pantry (1958), eggs and scales ready for Friday (baking day).

HOMAGE
TO THE HOUSE

The late summer of 1975 afforded some pleasant long afternoons to explore the land and buildings at Hartington. Pacing the ground led to the first plans and an appreciation of the actual shapes and proportions of the various parts. As soon as you have drawings on paper, you can begin to envisage something new. But it was on our first walk that we saw the policies we would pursue in each section. The new garden was born on that afternoon; we longed to be making it.

The thin strip at the front of the house bordering the lane would be a place of box hedges with some topiary. There could be simple herbaceous planting to be instantly cheerful but precedence would belong to the evergreens. The proportions of house and garden were very similar to those of Mary Arden's house and garden. I had also fallen in love with Levens, which is not much further from us than Edinburgh, and Marjorie had found one or two books on topiary which had inspired her to notes and drawings. She would like a hen, a 'speckled' hen, perhaps some of her beloved blackbirds, and barely twenty miles away we had found a huge thought-provoking peacock, if it was a peacock. It dwarfed, perhaps terrified, the little cottage beside it.

Then we walked around the east corner of the house. For the first time, we met the granary with its beautifully proportioned arches. Instantly we were transported to those monastic places and to the cloistered cathedral gardens which we had so liked. The small yard in front of the arches was partially enclosed within stone walls, while on the left was the stone barn. This was probably twelve feet high and sixty feet long. We knew that this almost enclosure would be a herb garden.

Although the barn was separate from the house, its east wall had been continued to join the house's north-east gable, and at that junction a fine stone doorway opened to a path between the buildings which led to the ground north of the house. However, we walked on between the barn and the granary and found a large open space. This was closed to the east by a dry-stone wall, to the south by the Hall's walled garden and ahead, to the north, by a 'sod cast' wall of soil encased in dark, blue-grey whinstones. Ridges of whin broke through the field surface further along the lane. Old sycamores grew through the sod cast.

A further, lower building had once joined the granary to the walled garden. The shape of its roof is deeply etched into the east gable, and the remains of its arch now form the south-east corner of the building. The demolition may have been recent and had been roughly executed, leaving wounds in the masonry at both ends. It had permitted the creation of a circular track from the farm cottages through the farmyard, passing granary and barn, to the Hall and the lane. We walked up to the north-east corner of the site where we found the sheep dip. The ground was covered with thick grass and nettles, but we could see that this would be the place to recreate Marjorie's nursery and fruit garden. There would also be space to create a car park for visitors.

Turning to the west we found a long piece of ground on the other side of the barn which stretched from the house to the sod cast. Further to the west the long sweep of Bert's newly created home and workshop was set off perfectly by mown grass and a small vegetable plot. There was no boundary; Bert stopped mowing in a line with his newly created garage in the low byre.

There were two further architectural features. A dilapidated dry-stone wall ran from the long sod cast down towards the north-west corner of the barn, which it once must have joined. Its lower end had also been roughly demolished to accommodate the farm track. Through our 'garden' the track was now concreted. Huge ill-fitting doors had been inserted into the barn's north gable, which must have allowed modern tractors to enter the eighteenth-century space. Where the wall now ended, a solitary telephone pole had been inserted. This carried Bert's line diagonally over our heads to his back door. It was a generous piece of land that would make a long flower garden, while we could grow shrubs on a further square area north of the track. So the new garden would have five parts including the nursery garden.

We also mused that both the farm track and the telephone pole would have to go, and that we might not want seven old sycamore trees.

Early twentieth-century gardening books addressing the problem of creating new country gardens, generally to accompany new country houses, advocated, without actually mentioning it, the Roman principle of *divide et impera* – divide and you will rule – used in governing the many provinces of their empire. This meant giving people different jobs and responsibilities so that everyone was absorbed and happy. Gardens needed the same treatment; each section needed to pursue separate policies. Our plant collection would divide accordingly. No plant would appear in more than one setting.

We had observed that some gardeners used favourite plants repeatedly. In small enclosures this could create potentially exciting patterning but in large areas repetition is soon boring. We had also noticed that while divisions could make a garden seem larger, having too many could be confusing, even claustrophobic. Fortunately, the southern and eastern parts were already satisfactory; we only needed to reorder the northern and western ones.

There was a further, very persuasive idea to be considered: the garden should be related to the house. No rules for achieving this ideal had been set out. But there were two hints, and these helped to shape our plans. In Renaissance gardens, architectural axes were created to link the house to the furthest parts of the design. A second hint lay in considering the age of the house. So, for example, a Georgian house would not be enhanced by a design typical of either earlier or later centuries.

We had seen the creation of a 'period' garden at Moseley. There you not only found a good Elizabethan house but also walked into the pages of Elizabethan gardening books. This was delightful. The approach at Wallington was different. Instead of reinstating period features, a modern garden exploring themes of contemporary interest was established within the existing framework.

The old Hartington farmhouse probably belonged to the sixteenth century, like Arch's Farm and the Stratford farms we had found so attractive. We certainly intended that the garden should pay due homage to the house. We could devise an axis in the flower area, but we were not academics given to historical research and exactitude. All life's adventures so far told us that we wanted to create a twentieth-century garden, not a perfectly accurate 'period' garden. Yet at the same time, in both design and contents, it should reflect the age of the house. Where there was no existing framework to work with, we would have to create all the boundaries and the internal structure. In doing this we would refer to the past. The planting of the spaces created would then be ours to experiment with.

Our plant collection could also contribute historical links. The four native evergreens – yew, box, ivy and holly – so memorable in the country churchyards, could be used as principal elements throughout the garden. These would have been very familiar to ancient gardeners. We now had a modestly wide selection of different forms of these which might create different effects of colour and light: ancient plants with modern accents. In supplementing them with other shrubs and climbers, we would employ forms of wild plants we enjoyed in the lanes: willows, elderberries, guelders and alder. There would be the climbing honeysuckles and forms of spindletree and a few of the useful old garden favourites which often appeared in northern gardens: jasmines, cotoneasters and barberry.

The themes we had chosen for the different parts were 'as old as time'. Topiary, the scents of the medicinal plants, the great joy of colour in a cold climate as expressed in both flower and foliage, and the fascination of pattern would all be established within a deliberately formal layout. And we guessed that the tighter the formal structure was, the greater the scope might be for an element of frivolity to creep in. Frivolity is humour and joy.

Herbaceous plants would need to be selected as rigorously as the shrubs. We thought that the first gardens, especially in the country, would have had to use wild flowers. Two aspects of these were especially interesting. The first concerned unusual, uncharacteristic forms, including double-flowered forms. These natural variations are probably more common than imagined, especially if you look. We had found a few and there were others long treasured in gardens. Then there were also the wild flowers from other parts of the country that are not normally found locally. They too would have been treasured and eagerly swapped. We once had a picnic in Worcestershire and found we were almost sitting on a 'Coventry Bell' (*Campanula trachelium*) flowering uncharacteristically low in the recently cut grass verge. The farmer's wife from Devon who gave us some *Allium triquetrum* complained that it invaded her lawn. Here it is lovely, and every spring we look forward to seeing it again. Climate makes a difference to a plant's behaviour. However, Marjorie always removes dead flowers to prevent seeding!

Early gardeners would also have enjoyed getting relatives of the natives from abroad when the first plant collectors brought their trophies home. We could grow these additional species too, but the florists' hybrids, particularly the ever larger and even more outrageously coloured recently created forms, might look out of place. If you like flowers it can be hard to say 'No,' but here we would probably want to.

The new garden would not resemble our Wallington one. It would not be a 'cottage' garden. It would be very organised, and the cottage ideal now seemed to us to embrace a strong element of chaos. Margery Fish was the fairy queen of cottage gardening, and yet her garden was incomprehensible. She had collected material not only from her humble 'cottage excursions' but from national botanic gardens and the greatest private gardens, including Sissinghurst, and somehow she had found spaces for everything. But order had not been a consideration. Valerie Finnis's fine photograph of her placed her in the only formal part, beside her row of fat clipped cones. This is a very satisfying picture.

In the book *Happy England*, the Helen Allingham watercolours were sophisticated, highly organised paintings, usually focused upon a cottage fairy. This was her daughter, who might, if necessary, have been chained to the spot for the sake of art. She reads a text, she looks with the intensity of wonder into flowers, she kneels beside them. The pictures were beautifully executed and coloured, and through late Victorian into Edwardian times they spread the cottage message.

Mrs Allingham could have painted some of the small square plots in our village in the 1960s; they still had something in common with the gardens she had found. They had their trophies, and their heirlooms, and all the joys that came out of forgotten packets of seeds someone had sown. These will always be a delight, but we were now faced with planting a large flower 'yard' which, in comparison, was like a small rectangular field. Indeed, memories of seeing Botticellis and ancient 'mille-fleur' tapestries prompted thoughts of trying to create a floral meadow, but one filled with 'garden' flowers: a space you could walk through as if by chance and meet flowers and be lost among them, both the very familiar and the unknown. This would require much thought.

We had looked at Gertrude Jekyll's planting plans. These were meticulously ordered drawings dealing with both the architecture of planting and the blending of colours. She saw her creations as paintings to be viewed from a distance as in an art gallery. At her own huge new 'cottage', Munstead Wood, the flower garden covered two acres out of the total of fifteen acres or more, and for this she kept a full-time gardening staff of fifteen. Out of sight, perhaps behind her great wall, there were reserved pots of plants waiting to be rushed in should any plant in the border suddenly fail. Perfection was to be maintained irrespective of nature. This would not be a method for us to follow.

Although we visited Hartington on quiet summer afternoons, we also came on other days. We had known occasional day-long gales at Wallington, for one of them had blown over two of our larger shrub roses, which offended our dignity, too. However, at Wallington the woods surrounding us on all but the east, which had just the noble oak tree, absorbed their ferocity and some of their noise. The Trust had undertaken a massive cull of elderly and potentially dangerous beeches which had lost Lady Pauline's grant of immunity. As a result, spaces and mounds that temporarily appeared in the old green haven could have been painted by Paul Nash, the war artist. Recovery was swift.

It was an astonishing experience for us to meet the westerly gale funnelling along the river valley at Hartington. It was not muffled and mitigated by woods, for there were none. It howled and shrieked at us and hurled its might against the barn and along the house, back and front. You had to creep along, almost touching the walls, hoping that the slates did not take flight. You could not stand to think, you had to escape. Now we knew why the barn had been carefully joined to the corner of the house. This simple device with a heavy door prevented some of the fury from reaching the granary front and its courtyard.

Betty's oft-quoted little rhyme explaining the nature of the different winds –

When the wind is in the north

The fishermen go not forth,

When the wind is in the east,

'Tis neither good for man nor beast,

When the wind is in the south,

It blows the bait into the fish's mouth,

When the wind is in the west,

It is at its very best

– conveyed simple truthful observations, but didn't fit occasional gales.

The lack of woods enabled us to see the wider landscape, something we had been unaware of at Wallington. We were at an elevation of almost seven hundred feet, probably similar to Wallington, for, as any cyclist will tell you, there are ups and downs in between. Although close to the bottom of the little river valley, there are still extensive views in each direction. Everywhere was green. There was no escaping this undulating greenery and we began to enjoy it. Quite oddly, we were going to be making a garden within this great 'Northumbrian lawn'.

Clearly, we needed shelter. Marjorie had now a good collection of yew and holly seedlings, already six inches high. In 1974 we had also unexpectedly indulged in a collection of shrubs, both large and small. This stock expansion had been occasioned by the sad closure of an ancient nursery in Morpeth. Matheson's had existed for over three hundred years. The last two brothers died in 1970 and 1974; there were, it was said, crippling death duties to be paid. Their acres had shrunk to fifty in 1947 after their father died, and after 1970 there only remained the land along the river beside their impressive house headquarters at the edge of town. The entrance to the site was distinguished by massive variegated hollies which protected the house from the winds travelling along that river valley.

We had spent many hours there exploring the collection. Where else could you then choose old and new shrub roses, find a dozen or more different forms of box, and see such different hollies, both green and variegated, and so many interesting shrubs? Every spring long thin beds of fine black soil were dug and planted with new tree seedlings and new propagations. Side paths still had box edging. For three centuries or more, this nursery had supplied the great estates of Northumberland. Sometimes, when visiting local gardens, we had been proudly told that shelter belts or formal shrub planting had been the work of Mr Matheson. He had a thoughtful and sensitive touch.

Suddenly, the site had to be cleared in limited time, because the land was to be 'developed' for housing. For us it seemed a tragic loss. The town was rightly proud of its fine park, and it and Matheson's nursery could almost have been joined to form a continuous garden at the river edge. However, there was no time for such thoughts.

We had always got on well with the foreman, who directed all the work with a hearty voice. The brothers were seldom seen on site except when discussing stock for orders. Now we could buy anything – small, large or enormous. It could be instantly dug up or we could dig it ourselves. Customers appeared with vans and trailers. It was the sale of centuries.

One huge trophy was the old stock plant of the 'corkscrew' hazel, then often called 'Harry Lauder's Walking Stick'. It could have been a hundred years old. It now guards one of the gates into the Hartington nursery. I had read that this form of hazel had been found in Gloucestershire in the nineteenth century. I could always imagine someone, perhaps out walking with a dog, coming upon this amazing sight, just as a century earlier someone had discovered the first 'Irish' yew in an Irish churchyard. Such legends, such strange natural variations or 'sports', are fascinating to gardeners. They are a subplot in our plant collection.

Unfortunately, root balls were always infested with ground elder and 'wicken', which we had called 'squitch' in the Midlands but is generally called 'couch-grass'. We had been told that since the 'gaffer' had died in 1947, they hadn't done any weeding. Before then, men lined up every morning, military style, to receive the day's orders, after which everyone had to dash off in all directions to make sure that no rogue weed had appeared overnight. Since then, standards had been relaxed.

Every trace of soil had to be combed out of the roots and every fragment of the enemies removed. Top growth had to be well cut back. In spite of the season and all the bashing and shaking, the specimens accepted their treatment and 'lived happily ever after'.

Many small new propagations in pots were bought too. Thanks to this invasion of new material and Marjorie's own propagating, it seemed we were well equipped for the new garden.

An old friend in a nearby village reported the existence of a young man named Dick who was said to do construction work. He lived, possibly in a caravan, beside a farm, up a long track, off a narrow road – a route never explored. The telephone was better. It seemed that he possessed all manner of equipment, a JCB, tractor or tractors, and also 'had a man'. Some prods with a fork confirmed that our 'garden' was a properly stoned farmyard disguised under years of neglect which had produced a strong ground cover of weeds.

His enthusiasm to tackle our job spilled out of him; there were many puffs from his pipe as he stroked his beard. For a thousand pounds, he would de-stone the land, plough it, rotovate it, spread whatever soil and manure we could find over it, level it, and in six months we would have our new garden.

Our work for 1976 was now set out. Entry to Hartington was agreed for immediately after Easter. On Tuesday, after the Bank Holiday, the barn's great doors were open to receive the first deliveries of building materials. For that long hot summer all our newly acquired land belonged to the builder.

Ernie had been the Wallington joiner, Bill's companion for many a lunchtime in the courtyard. He had a good understanding of structure, and ambition. He now employed a dozen craftsmen. The Trust's agent took great interest in what we were doing, for it was the first time such a lease had been granted. He called in regularly to see the progress and his opinions were valued. Every evening Ernie and I discussed the day's achievements.

At some mutually convenient point in the autumn, Dick would arrive to begin his work. Before then I would weed-kill all the ground. This required a dozen or more hundredweights of sodium chlorate, bought from an old chemist's shop in Hexham, which I applied dry, by hand. The hot summer now favoured us. One application was sufficient; since there was no rain, the weeds never recovered. Before autumn, the whole site was as dry and bare as a desert.

Our garden at Wallington had to be reordered for the sake of whoever might live there next, for it would be most unlikely that they would be garden enthusiasts. The flower garden, the 'cottage' garden, was simplified. Important plants were propagated or occasionally removed, to create the herbaceous stocks needed for Hartington. The grass was removed from the lawned area and dug in to make a vegetable garden.

The required plants were then transferred to our Wallington allotment. They could not invade our nursery, which had to be retained. It would have to continue to function until the new one had been created. During the autumn and the winter beyond, whatever could be packed indoors would be prepared and the new house would be decorated.

It seemed to be the busiest of years. Somehow all the sunshine kept us going.

Above: the original farmhouse and byre as found in 1975.
Opposite: the 'euphoric plan' conceived in 1975.
Following page: *Lilium lancifolium* var. *fortunei*.

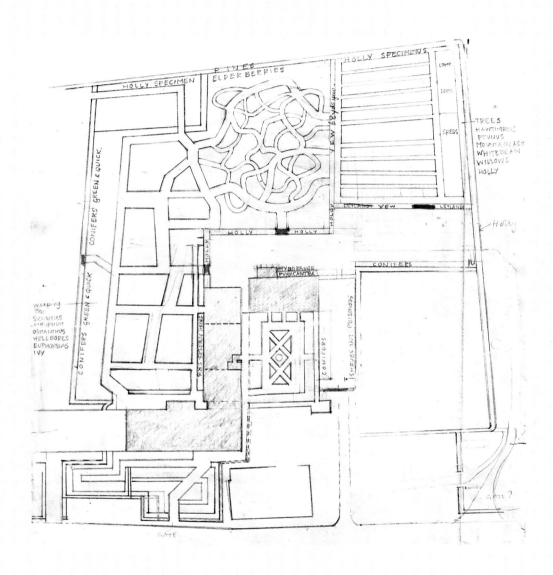

Part Three

THE NEW GARDEN

ASPECTS OF GARDEN CONSTRUCTION

The three site problems we wished to resolve took varying amounts of time; one phone call dislodged the telephone pole; the removal of the farm track was partially accomplished in a few months but not completed for five years; the dripping sycamore trees lasted for three years.

It was essential to create a west boundary before Dick's garden excavations could begin. Bert marked the edge of his grass-cutting ambitions, and we were happy to have a generous width of garden corresponding to the width of the house, and a generous area beyond to grow a double shelter belt. Bert understood the need for shelter at Hartington.

A quick glance at our surrounding landscape told us that the proper way to create a boundary was to build a wall. Walls, seldom seen in the landscape at Wallington, were everywhere. They were so much more practical than posts and rails, or wires, for they were permanent. Walls looked perfectly at home in the open hills, following contours as happily as grass or heather or sheep. We are barely twenty miles north of the perfect Roman model.

The old masons had been so skilful in making everything life required in stone. Farms and fields not only had walls but there would also be troughs of varying sizes, some carved from massive boulders over six feet long with chiselled sides four inches thick, some might only be a foot long or less, and some, large and small, were round. Some tiny round ones with carved appendages could be cressets, primitive Saxon oil lamps as in Hexham Abbey. If they had served a pump, they could have a square back and a decorative half-round front and be only one inch thick. There were square, round or octagonal upright vessels with thick bottoms which had been mortars or, some said, domestic cheese presses. These survived in gardens, near a door, where they might house a marigold. There would be a hole at the back, just above the bottom, for drainage. They were probably discarded in better places when the round white marble mortars, which looked so hygienic, became fashionable. These had lugs which lodged them securely into tree-trunk bases. All these had begun to find new homes in gardens.

There was now a new purpose for the oddly angled old wall: it could be rebuilt as part of that west boundary. We needed more stone, and we needed a waller. Wall building was an aspect of garden construction we had not anticipated.

While we had admired the Wallington garden walls, we had never for a moment thought of putting ourselves into the shoes of those who had built them, or pondered that, until they had been built, a garden could not have been made inside them. Nor did we foresee the extent of wall building that awaited us at Hartington.

I asked the National Trust agent for help. Again he responded positively. There was quite a length of long ruined wall, sometimes little more than foundations dug a foot into the ground, on a hillside behind one of the Wallington farms, just beyond the western edge of the woods. We would have to dig it out and repair the landscape. No trace of either the ruin or our visit should remain.

He helped us enormously by providing the manpower to accomplish this. Any thoughts we may have had that, after Dick's ground preparations, we would manage to make the garden on our own were already thoroughly challenged.

Had we thought of applying to set up a Job Creation Project? I am not good at following politics and current affairs, so I certainly had not. This scheme was not available to private enterprise, but since we were leasing land from the National Trust, he was convinced an application would succeed. He was right and we were granted three workers including a supervisor.

The buzz of small motorbikes bringing the boys from Morpeth became a feature of life. They were allowed a six-month job, while our supervisor, Tommy, was allowed twelve months. He had been at school with Marjorie, one of Miss Thompson's team of boys who attended to the vegetables, while the girls looked after the flowers. He kept a neat village garden. His allegiance was to the vegetables and bedding plants school. His summer holidays had been spent helping on the farm at Hartington. He had loved that time, and retained a good memory of the site of the drains which ran through and served our land. Having driven the travelling shop which served the village branch of the 'Co-op' for twenty-two years, he had just been made redundant when it closed. His help was extremely useful.

Technically, I became the 'employer'. I received no pay but I collected the tax and National Insurance contributions, kept perfect records submitted for monthly inspection, and issued proper wage packets every Thursday. The workers received agricultural rates of pay, graded according to age and, in the case of the supervisor, responsibility. In addition to wages, there was a small allowance to provide necessary tools, and to cover occasional extra expenses such as the hire of an old tractor and trailer and a farmer's son. Now we could both dig and 'lead' stone.

We had already managed to get a bit of walling done. On the only day we spent away that summer, a lingering visit deep into Cumbria, we called to see the Hartington house on our way home, after nine o'clock. A huge heap of stone, not previously there, now lay at the front door. In our absence there had been a disaster. The three-foot-thick wall of boulder stones which had separated house from byre, from floor to roof, had collapsed. Bert later described the sudden terrifying noise. A labourer, attempting to dislodge an old oak lintel so that a wide doorway could be inserted to allow internal passage between the two sections, had unfortunately dislodged everything else.

The old wall had once housed two fireplaces. Their jambs and lintels had long ago been stolen or removed. The great holes had remained unrepaired. You could look up beautifully built flues to the slates that now closed them. The chimney had gone too. After consultation with the architect, all remains of the wall were removed and carried outside. It was a great shock, and a great disappointment. We had planned to repair and retain that most characterful feature.

But now stone was to hand in front of the house to provide a low enclosing wall for the hedge and topiary garden. We consulted Marjorie's Uncle Norman, a fine stonemason. His summers were spent working on Hadrian's Wall and his winters in the wonderful but draughty Aydon Castle. He had cleaned, repaired and dressed the fireplaces we had unearthed in our cottage at Wallington.

Too ill to offer us physical help, he warned of difficulties in getting a waller. A government subsidy was being paid to farmers and public bodies such as the National Parks for the repair of their old walls. Much of Northumberland is National Park: all the wallers were very busy. However, he did know a well-intentioned farm worker who 'did a bit'.

Jimmy would tidy and fill gaps in the fell walls in winter at the farm where he worked. He was very willing and clearly pleased that Norman should have put his name forward, but he had never built a new wall, even a low one, before. The builder's labourers were amused by him. He was very 'out by', tall and awkward, shy and slow in speech, but very determined to do his job. He was not used to their constant banter – 'Tell him to put some cement in the mixer . . .' But his little walls are solid and still here, now covered by ivy. He also managed to build the short missing section of enclosing wall for the yard in front of the granary. His contribution was valuable.

Now, a little later, with a major wall to build, we consulted Norman again. This was a 'serious waller's' job. 'I think you could try Sid, he's got a new apprentice. He'll likely come the mornday.' (That is, tomorrow.) Old Sid was now multi-dimensional thanks to his highly talented apprentice, who really had little to learn; he could take on two jobs at once. He inspected the stone we had collected, and sent us Arthur Rogerson.

By the time we saw Sid again, all he had to do was to present the bill. Arthur, whose previous career in building had made him expert at banter, consumed stone and turned it into fine walling as compulsively and effortlessly as I had watched Betty on winter evenings consuming wool. From her dancing needles came men's socks, three pairs for each of her 'menfolk' for Christmas, and possibly gloves. Six yards a day came from Arthur's simple wooden frame and constantly readjusted strings.

If this was accomplished before half past five he would do some more. The labourer carried stone for him, laid it out for inspection, controlling the supply. The discarded was removed into a heap, then broken and stored for later use as central filling.

A stone was lifted into the left hand, its face and shape adjusted by the small square 'mash' hammer, then placed exactly. It might require a tiny stone wedge at a corner. The stone would always be 'right', and it led into perfect secondary contours judged aesthetically as patterns within the form. Periodically, building stopped and the filling was tipped in, levelled with a finger. It was like a cook filling a giant pie case. When necessary, a large stone was cut into two or four 'builders', with a few blows with a heavy 'mell' hammer. These cut perfectly. Regularly, a large 'jumper' was inserted to add deliberate height and weight, and halt the rising or falling contours. They were part of the aesthetic structure too. At three stages the wall was levelled, its width carefully checked and a layer of cement added, tying the sides over the filling. This happened at the foundation, half-way, and below the coping stones. If none were provided, new 'copes' were made. A stone was cut to the exact width and its top deftly rounded.

The stone's familiar weathered grey colour was constantly chiselled away by the cutting and hammering so that the newly finished wall glowed with the warm natural colour. In three years driving rain, which has free access to the dry-stone wall, will grey it again. But in this very pure air, lichens will soon decorate like sequins, moss will gather at the 'copes' and the middle band, and small patches of yellow, red, olive and black will appear.

In long winters, while the flowers sleep, a walled garden becomes a garden of walls, a simpler more sculptural place. Walls full of colour also reflect the good waller's passionate judgement of shapes and contours; they are his artistic compositions. They vie with your evergreens and topiaries for your attention.

Replacing the sod cast with high dry-stone walls was a big job. The sycamores had huge boles, some of which were too heavy and awkward to lift into a trailer. They had to lie for three years until dry enough to be broken into smaller pieces. The great discovery was finding that the sod cast was the old farmer's hoard of topsoil removed so carefully from all but the nursery area of the garden. It was a labour of love to patiently wheel it all back. A lot of whinstones came too, but these provided the base of the new access road which replaced the eastern end of the farm track. Time has a marvellous way of solving problems for you if you will trust it.

The site of the new access road had been elusive. Plans to enter via the field to the east had been frustrated by a feature known as the 'saucer'. Centuries earlier, lead had been mined at Hartington. This had provided gutters and drainpipes for Wallington. The disturbed field surface near the houses told of spoil heaps while the 'saucers' (there were others too) are the tops of shafts. One had opened up overnight beside the hall fifty years earlier and was alleged to have been thirty feet deep.

The solution was to make a new drive through the eastern edge of the Hall's walled garden. In exchange for this extra land, we engaged Arthur to construct a new garden wall for which the Trust provided the stone. Arthur was then able to construct a wall to close off the farm track too. The area of track left on our side became our 'materials yard' for the storage of stone, soil and hardcore. A few years later a previously unsuspected shaft appeared just inside the Hall garden. The ground subsided two feet, leaving a few yards of Arthur's new wall suspended in space. Inevitably it collapsed, and he rebuilt it after the shaft was properly sealed. Luck had been on our side.

It was astonishing to see how much hardcore Dick's de-stoning work produced. The heap covered much of the area of the present car park with boulders and every possible smaller size too. Much was used in constructing the present garden paths, while I selected hand-sized stones to edge all the borders and beds to hold soil back from the paths. It was believed that until the early nineteenth century a paved Roman way, a branch of the 'Devil's Causeway', had crossed the river, possibly by the stepping stones. Did I select some of their stones? Had the ever-practical farmers found a new purpose for the relics?

By late autumn the site began to look very respectable. If our ambition for the garden had coincided with Dick's possible vision, which we had never discussed, we could have ordered huge quantities of grass seed. By spring we might have achieved an estate agent's dream of 'beautifully landscaped grounds'.

Instead we began the task of carefully laying out, in turn, each section of the garden. First, the ground had to be levelled. Stakes were inserted at regular intervals, north to south, east to west, and strings were tied to them as tightly as possible. This process instantly revealed high and low places, and soil was raked to the strings.

Our greatest feat of levelling was the car park, now defined by one of Arthur's walls. It was excavated, filled and rolled. For the garden paths, we had acquired a small old garden roller from a local sale. But this great area was an altogether more daunting prospect. Then, in line with all the other magic Hartington had somehow evoked to aid the construction of this garden, a mysterious visitor called on a Friday afternoon. For the only known time, the little lane was being tarmacked. This man was in charge of the great roller. 'Excuse me, mate, do you know anywhere I could leave the roller out of sight, off the road, for the weekend?' I did, but there would be a price. Before it could be released, it would need to roll a few times over the car park. For a man who worked on his own, that would not present any difficulty. 'See you Monday,' he said. The car park then became a real asset. It was the ideal place to deposit loads of stone. When it was full, Arthur was recalled.

Stakes and strings marked the paths, which were carefully measured. The Victorian expert, Mrs Earle, discussed the importance of due consideration of path widths. She was a great supporter of the cottage garden movement, but clearly worked in larger gardens too. Stress was laid upon function, with main paths being twice as wide as secondary ones, while avenues should accommodate at least three walking side by side in comfort. Apart from paved terraces either side of the house, we had no avenues, and decided to make main paths three feet six inches wide, and the others two feet.

Our soil cover was not great. Soil could not be wasted in paths, especially when we had such a quantity of hardcore, so it was dug out to a depth of almost twelve inches and deposited on the beds the paths defined. Dick had scraped a layer from the designated nursery, the only section not covered by farmers' hardcore, and had spread it all over the whole site. We had also managed to acquire some soil and a local farmer had given two generous loads of manure as a welcoming present.

Paths were filled with stone. Into the bottoms went roughly broken boulders, then a middle filling, and then a topping of finely broken pieces. From Bill's old tool collection came 'mells' for the boulders and a variety of hand hammers for topping. Our team had now been increased to six, two girls and four boys, and provided varying combinations of excavators, stone breakers and barrowers. After I had edged all the beds they were double dug in the old manner: the top spit put to the back of the bed, the second spit dug and the top spit of the next row put forward on to the second spit. Once a section of the garden was completed, everyone could see that, though it lacked plants, it looked very much better, even 'special'.

Hartington's ancient history added an independent interest to the subsoil. One of the earliest ladies of the Hall, when all of Hartington was still called 'Herterton', was a legend. She was 'Meg o' Meldon'. Meldon lies six miles to the east but was connected to Hartington by the now lost secret underground passage. Her ghost appears both in the Hall and on the bridge over the Hart at Meldon, beside the ancient 'Keeper's Cottage'. The keeper looked after the adjoining deer park. Meg was a miser and, in that time of border raids and murderous cattle thieves, buried her treasure. She is still looking for it. We were both gardeners and treasure-seeking archaeologists.

We found a few old coins, glass and pottery marbles, clay pipe fragments and horseshoes of widely different shapes and sizes. The clearly ancient 'Saxon' spoon was buried near a doorway. It was 'barnacled' with rust. Heavily patterned, possibly with an inscription, it needed a lot of scrubbing. Eventually, it became legible: 'Made in England'.

The soil texture was improved by the addition of local peat. Marjorie's middle brother, Alan, lived six miles away in an old farmhouse surrounded by untold acres of forestry trees. He and his wife led a heroic life of bringing up their family in deep isolation by farming a hundred scattered acres of variable quality. They were 'scrattin' about' too. A visit entailed driving for five miles on forestry tracks over unseen hills and valleys. Occasionally areas of forest were harvested and then the unique Northumberland landscape stretching away to the Cheviots was revealed.

The huge forestry draining machines, which maintained roads and prepared planting sites, set up high dykes of peat. After drying summers, these became enviable mounds of evenly textured material. Alan arranged a meeting with the forestry man in his office beside the neat forestry workers' village.

There were two questions: could we dig and buy some, and would he have use for a load or two of our seemingly endless supply of hardcore? He was a very pleasant man. A price was agreed, and it was 'Yes' to the hardcore. We were lucky. The new draining machines can shred and cast the peat back on to the land as it is dug.

Alan was very thrifty, and kept an endless store of fertiliser and feeder bags. The spade cut neat slices of dry peat and, when filled, the bags had little weight. Alan and his old tractor and trailer were hired for the transport. Our team enjoyed their occasional days in that pristine wild environment. Once, to suit Alan, everyone came in on a Saturday, happily accepting Monday as a long 'lie-in' day in exchange. We worked in an open tree-felled area with extensive views, filling and carrying sacks through tree stumps and over ditches to the waiting trailer. The sun sent grey shadows racing over the landscape and over our feet from the flying banks of high May clouds. It was Cup Final day and, far from civilisation, someone's little transistor radio kept us in touch with the score.

The sacks were stacked under the granary arches and on snowy or frosty days were unpacked and the peat hand-shredded and barrowed outside. When digging resumed in better weather, it was mixed into the soil. On other wintry days we sat or knelt in the same place and knapped stone, making heaps of path topping.

It was sad when we learnt that the Job Creation Project scheme was to end nationally at Christmas 1979. We held our last Christmas party. With four old trestles and two old doors, a refectory table was created upstairs in the granary. Since this was to become our future 'lecture room', we had chipped the old whitewash from the walls and had added a simple white-painted ceiling following the slates up to the ridge. One of our 'boys', Bob, had had some experience in the building trade and had developed great skill in pointing. Inside and outside, those walls are testimony to his ability and patience. He was always Arthur's principal labourer.

Marjorie found tablecloths. She is the best of sandwich makers, and we bought cream cakes and other delights. We had a very large green enamelled 'factory' teapot and Staffordshire earthenware dishes of the not-quite-perfect sort you could then find in Newcastle in the short-lived pottery cellars which appeared in the seventies. We preferred them to the 'better' sets available in respectable stores. The girls got everything ready, carried it, and laid the table. It seemed almost medieval in style. It may not have been our first party, but it was the best. The December darkness was almost complete when the last motor and motorbike drove away. For over three years we had done a lot of work together, and done it very thoroughly.

Now the stone-gathering team was reduced to Alan and me, and on a long July day, lasting until seven o'clock, we could accomplish three trips. Marjorie provided a hearty lunch after we returned with the first load. In total we would bring in twelve tons. Our radius for collecting never exceeded eleven miles, which Alan judged the safety limit of his little old cabless tractor. It really did a great deal of work for us. It took eight years to complete the walls, and Arthur later calculated that we had used 700 tons of stone. On the occasional night in the pub, Arthur's trained ear would detect through the swirling conversations the slightest hint that some farmer might be struggling a little, and might have a little stretch of derelict wall to spare . . .

By Easter in 1980, the final tractor-load of huge 'Matheson' shrubs arrived from Wallington, with enormous yews and hollies. It was perhaps a joke that it had taken more than three years to move us and our plant collection just three miles. The first planting of the garden was completed later that summer.

In the demolition-mad eighties, you might, once or twice, have seen another of Alan's assets, an old blue hard-worked truck with a tipping back, deep in the old suburbs of Newcastle or Gateshead. I would be with Alan in the cab, and you might have spotted Arthur too. There would be stone chisels, mells, iron crowbars and spikes somewhere in the back. By then the garden had told us it was time to improve the house to keep pace with its surroundings. Their relationship had to be tightened. We were hunting domestic stone. Demolition proceeded at a great pace. In limited time, everything would be crushed. New domestic or industrial estates would arise. You had to respond quickly to the whispers.

It was a privilege to work with these men whose common sense unlocked ancient secrets. Moving great shrubs too heavy to lift and carry, huge stone troughs which a team of men could not lift and carry, and installing massive stone lintels and fireplaces downstairs and upstairs, was all in a day's work.

When Alan so sadly died in 2012, he was the last surviving member of Sir Charles's workforce. After school, he became the Wallington joiner's apprentice and helped to make and install the wonderful gate opening from the courtyard on to the west lawn. He then, like us, followed new ambitions and calling, but it was his old skill that made us doors and gates for the garden and the barn.

Top left: servant lad and servant lass near milking time (date unknown).
Top right: the decrepit state of the granary in 1975.
Bottom left: de-stoning the Physic Garden with Dick.
Bottom right: Arthur building the first section of high wall, served by Bob.

Opposite: Marjorie and Zac preparing the site of a willow at the edge of the car park.
Above left: Alan and the job creation team hand loading surplus hardcore for delivery to the forest.
Above right: our final Christmas party together in 1979.

THE PICTURE
IN THE FRAME

The removal van arrived on the last day of February 1977. After breakfast the following morning, Marjorie, as usual, took breadcrumbs out of the back door into the garden. It was a great surprise to find that no birds were waiting. There would have been a great crowd at Wallington. In such cold weather even the woodpecker would have forsaken the trees for a few moments and flown up to join the company. Here, the door opened into emptiness. There was not a single bush on which a bird could perch and peer at us while we might peer back. No door had opened here with breadcrumbs for at least one, and perhaps two, hundred years, and in that old stackyard of stones not even an elderberry could have flourished.

From inside we now looked into the 'flower' garden, the heart of the garden. It was drab and dull, without feature, without even a bird. Marjorie loved to work in the company of birds, and sometimes talked to them. While the ground preparations made their daily progress, she found time to sit at the table with her drawing board making notes and sketches; she was planning the planting. Outer shelter was the first necessity, and inside that an inner framework of shrubs was required, both to protect and to enhance the flowers. These would come last; they would be the picture within the frame.

Wise artists may fix a frame to the pristine white canvas before it is attached to the easel. The magic of art then allows frame and picture to grow together. The frustration of the painter who completes a picture but then cannot find either a frame or framer is avoided. There is a counterpoint between flowers and their surroundings which should guarantee both contrast and sympathetic support.

Mr Matheson knew how to make shelter. Native wind-resistant trees would come first, then 'garden' trees, and then shrubs in a balanced mixture of evergreen and deciduous specimens. While the west side bed we had waiting might have looked very wide while empty, we knew that ideals would have to be greatly compromised: the outer tree section had to be sacrificed. Instead, Marjorie chose to make a single outer barrier of holly, with a single line of potentially large shrubs inside.

There had been very little space on the west edge of Matheson's nursery to shelter the house and offices. They had a single defence of fine tall hollies, among which we particularly admired *Ilex x altaclerensis* 'Lawsoniana'. We knew a strong and long holly field hedge in the Borders, and had always admired the huge imperious holly trees we had found in many local lanes. Their early winter berry harvest brings the chortling mistlethrushes whose passion for them equals ours.

Large green-leaved specimens from Matheson's were duly planted inside Arthur's new wall along the west side of the garden. The most successful have proved to be two American hollies with large prickly leaves, which are now quite as big as the barn on the other side of the flower garden. As if as an afterthought, they can produce a few sombre dark red berries in the spring, which are seldom noticed. Least successful were the especially handsome, freely fruiting 'altaclerensis' hybrids. Their unknown parentage endowed them with long glossy dark green leaves without prickles. They have not liked the west winds; they should have had tree shelter. One has been replaced, and two others have been underplanted with native aquifolium seedlings. These are now often found in the garden, though sometimes they are flourishing all too well inside evergreen shrubs, where birds have paused to enjoy their stolen berries. The line was completed with three natives which have done well, one providing contrasting yellow fruit.

Perhaps moving at that dead time of year, so cold and inhospitable, gave Marjorie a brave and bold inspiration. Weather forecasts suggest that our temperatures are generally five degrees lower than in southern places, and winter often seems quite unreasonably the longest season, greedily trying to eliminate both spring and autumn. Regardless of the colour of our sky or the figures on the thermometer, she decided to create our own local sunshine. The 'frame' on both sides of the garden would concentrate on gold or yellow foliage, or yellow flowers, or yellow or white foliage variegation of all the shrubs, small trees and foliage carpets; the same for the climbers chosen to clothe the barn walls. Everything would radiate heat.

We knew that long ago the Impressionist painters had evolved a new technique using short brush strokes of bright colour to analyse and communicate the beauty of French sunshine and to examine the rich depths of its complementary shadows. Their yellows and pinks seemed particularly expressive of sunlight. It is not an accident that the largest flower bed, nearest to the house windows, is dominated by pink flowers.

At both ends of the 'golden' frame inside the hollies, a small tree adds height to the corners. At the southern end the larger one arches over to connect the house to the now high dark green hollies. This is the golden alder, *Alnus incana* 'Aurea'. In addition to its warm golden leaves, it provides a bounty of coral pink catkins in winter, which compensate us handsomely after the mistlethrushes have gorged on the holly berries. And should the catkins attract a marauding group of passing bullfinches, we can enjoy seeing them too. Close to the northern corner is a golden nut tree. Against the dark American hollies behind, this brings a shock of light lemon yellow.

The house's north side was planted with two very large leaved ivies, one with cream, one with yellow variegated foliage. Marjorie concealed the junction of house and bothy behind what is now a huge pyramid of 'Golden Queen' holly, a non-fruiting male form, rather unsuitably named. The alder manages to join this to its partner, an equally high cone of berrying golden holly planted on its other flank. This is answered at the nut tree end by one of a pair of Lawsoniana hollies. These belong to the group of golden 'splash' hollies whose leaves have a splash of yellow inside a green edge rather than the more usual green leaf with a yellow margin. All the 'splash' ones produce branches of entirely green foliage too, so that overall they present a darker shade of yellow, a green gold relieved with bright speckles. The twin towers of Lawsoniana hollies are separated by a now abandoned path lined with a shaped tree-box hedge. This once allowed Bert to wheel in his great old over-spilling wooden wheelbarrow, loaded with grass cuttings, to our compost heap. For half its length, the path's sides have joined. Is what is left of the blocked path now a 'folly'? An antique dealer friend, with a very good eye, recommends a sculpture, but that might be a distraction. It is a little mystery. Then the second Lawsoniana is joined by a yellow-flowered berberis, a yellow-leaved 'guelder rose' and a fine tall yellow variegated philadelphus named 'Innocence'. This was a gift from Doris, a widow who, for as long as she lived, kept her little twenty-acre farm of apples and plums near the River Teme, in that wonderfully fertile valley between Ludlow and Worcester. She liked flowers, but whatever we took her never seemed adequate compensation for a box of Victorias and, joys of joys, that most remarkable of 'cookers', 'Peasgood's Nonsuch', nonesuch indeed. The border is edged with ribbons of yellow-leaved raspberry, seldom growing even eighteen inches high, the warm gold of golden meadow-foxtail (*Alopecurus pratensis* 'Aureus'), with attractive flowers which should not be allowed to seed, and the brilliant light yellow of golden marjoram. The 'carpet' then climbs to a low-clipped yellow 'privet' and a pair of bright yellow Japanese box cubes, placed at either end of one of Arthur's stone benches. This itself wears a thin jacket of clipped yellow ivy. Then there is a pair of variegated periwinkles, and the line ends with a wide, rounded golden alpine 'currant'. A surprise is the pair of yellow Mlokosewitschii peonies in front of the Lawsoniana hollies. They were given to us by Miss Marigold B., who lived in rustic splendour in a small Elizabethan house in Westmorland. She knew a lot about horses, and loved her vegetable plot, and was very proud of her 'Molly the Witch' peonies, and she was generous.

The barn on the other side was a headache. Although we had tackled many jobs and tried many plants in the first garden, dealing with walls and climbing plants had not been attempted. It was so high and so long. There were no windows for relief, just a pair of widely separated doorways. The juxtaposition of its sheer vertical surface with the still unrelieved horizontal ground surface was confrontational.

Marjorie's plan was again *divide et impera*; she would insert strong verticals which would eventually cut that surface into separate compartments. We had seen how Graham Thomas had dealt with the much longer and equally high portico wall at Wallington which almost seemed stranded, nearly absorbed by the wood. The trees on the other side of the path were cut back, and a double line of tall conifers was planted at regular intervals. This perfectly bridged the gap between wall and wood, and rhythmically punctuated the walk.

Our task was not quite the same. Three golden yews and a fruiting golden holly, 'Golden King' – in fact a female form – were planted, as two pairs, either side of the doorways. The northern door, almost at the centre of the garden, had the pair of yews with the purpose of becoming a major, architectural distraction. They have grown into a gold tree porch, almost a 'triumphal arch,' five or six feet deep. The wide low door simply leads into the garage, home to all the everyday tools, forks, spades, shears, secateurs, brushes, and is very useful. It does have lovely wide gritty jambs, and may be worthy of the grand theatrical treatment. The other doorway became a window with the holly on its left and the other yew on its right. These became 'buttresses' making bridges between the garden and the building. The wall spaces in between were clothed in evergreen foliage, mostly euonymus and ivy, with a pair of the old 'glory' roses, the Victorian 'Gloire de Dijon', either side of the central section. Only one now survives, the other replaced by euonymus. Next Marjorie added a meandering horizontal contour of medium and small shrubs: spirea, philadelphus, miniature berberis and potentilla. At ground level, the planting was completed with bulbs, two more variegated grasses, and some bulky herbaceous plants not required for the flower beds. As a surprise for any early visitors, and a treat for us, the long 'golden' borders on both sides were given a blue edging. The first part to appear, on the barn side, is a line of tiny cobalt-blue *Chionodoxa sardensis*. The other side answers a week or so later, with a small bright-blue, white-centred form of *Chionodoxa luciliae* found in a garden near Jedburgh. With luck, the blues briefly overlap.

The low gate giving access from the car park is half-way between the barn and the yew hedge. You will glimpse the garden over it as you approach. On either side of it Arthur built a high wall. The contrast between our high walls and those at Wallington, which are similar in height to the barn walls, is striking. Ours are half as high and yet, in this much smaller space, they manage to look 'high' too. The relationship of ground space to wall height is critical. Wallington walls would have imprisoned us, and denied our visual escape into the landscape.

Marjorie planted another pair of golden yews either side of the gate in order to grow a second arch. Comparison between the two arches is now instructive. The 'porch' arch, backed by the barn and its high roof, is the 'triumph' indeed. The 'gate' arch is fully exposed to the winds, east and west, and is distinctly smaller. Its 'lintel', which rises fully two feet above the wall, is still not completely formed. Winds funnel between the barn gable with its 'extension', the granary, and trees and shrubs which edge the nursery wall opposite to them. Shelter protects for just so far, and then the wind swoops in.

The yellow theme continues up to the yew hedge, the 'stop' being a column of clipped golden 'Irish' yew, which has a partner on the other side close to the nut tree. They answer the pair of green columns close to the house. There is a variegated weigela to the left of the gate and a golden philadelphus to the right, and there is just room for a potentilla on each side too.

As soon as the shrubs were planted, the birds knew; the word spread. The garden seems to have become something of a hostel for birds. Old stalwarts came back, but these are wider skies. Our proximity to the moors has brought new faces to the garden, if not always to the breakfast table. We do not see our old woodpecker but hear his relative, the green one, hard at work in the copse nearby. And occasionally when you drive slowly along the lane he may fly in his very odd way ahead of you between the ash trees. He glides up and down crossing from one side to the other. It is the gait of someone who has tarried too long in the tavern. We can watch the heron come to do some fishing in the river, and surely there is no better sound or sight than the curlew passing over.

The design of the flower beds was created on the ground. Any diagonal paths, visible in the euphoric sketch plan of 1975, were eliminated out of respect for the buildings. The long rectangular plot, stretching from the house to the yew hedge, defined by the wide main paths around it, was divided by narrow paths across its width. This made four beds. Their proportions were deliberately varied, but not symmetrically. From the house they are thin, fat, not so thin, not so fat.

The four horizontal beds were then divided into three parts vertically by narrow paths. This time the outer pair were made equal, but the relationship of centre to each of its flanking beds was deliberately varied. From the house, the first, 'thin' bed has a centre very little wider than its flanks, while the second, 'fat' section has the widest of the centres, which is made into a square with two narrow flanks. The third, 'not so thin' section reverses this by having its centre bed narrower than its flanks, and the fourth, 'not so fat' part has a centre wider than its flanks, like the second section, but the proportions are not so extreme. However, in the fourth and final section there is another variation. The flanking beds turn towards each other top and bottom and so enclose the centre, which becomes a square within a rectangle. Access to the square is made by short central paths. In contrast to the outer wide paths around the garden, the inner route around the beds by which you can meet and examine the flowers is a deliberate meander of offset junctions which slowly draw you up from the house and into the centre.

The central axis, through the garden and the yew hedge into the garden beyond, is emphasised by a series of stone troughs and a sundial. These were implanted next. The four troughs are all circular and, for added emphasis, three are raised on circular plinths. The final marker is a simple Georgian sundial of 1746 with a square chamfered column supporting a square moulded head. So many of our early visitors had an irrepressible compulsion to walk directly into the flower bed where it was placed, regardless of soil and flowers, to see what time it was, that we 'temporarily' removed its dial; it was put somewhere indoors for 'safekeeping', The sundial is now more useful since, apart from marking the axis (its primary role), in times of occasional drought, when leaves are yellowing and flowers show stress, it is the perfect place, undisturbed by a gnomon, to place the sprinkler.

The composition of squares and rectangles marked by a grid of narrow pink sand paths, enlivened by central circles and one tiny square, pays homage to our love of the twentieth-century 'abstract' painters Piet Mondrian and Ben Nicholson.

The first three beds, nearest to the house, the smallest ones, were given an architectural role as part of the frame. Arthur built up the sides of the outer ones two feet, so that extra soil could be provided for a pair of green Irish yews, which are clipped into flat-topped columns. Miss Jekyll's very small form of white periwinkle fills in the top surface, and the surrounding low walls were planted with a miniature form of green euonymus which is clipped too. In case the arrangement should begin to look too formal, the little periwinkle is most efficient in deflating the situation. It raises itself into pyramids of new growth, some of which cascades freely over the edges, while some climbs ambitiously into the yews. These yews have most unexpected white flowers peeping out of their neat sides two or even three feet above ground if you are here in May.

The centre bed is one of Marjorie's miniature gardens within a garden. At the centre the raised trough is planted with a very small gold variegated saxifraga of the London Pride group, with white, pink-centred flowers. The plinth is planted with a slow-growing green ivy of the 'Saggitifolia' type, with typical long green deeply cut leaves. Its fingers clutch both trough and column. It is clipped twice, and keeps a neat respectful line two inches below the top edge of the trough. Around the base is a generous square of the gold-spotted form of London Pride with the usual pale flesh-pink flowers. Both saxifrages erupt together into fountains of palest pink throughout June, and are then severely trimmed. The sides of the London Pride are kept in order by a narrow eight-inch-wide path of stone, which, of course, allows you to trim the ivy around the trough comfortably. The other edge of these miniature paths is planted with a bulkier 'mossy' saxifrage with quite tall white flowers lasting into June, which was given to us by Graham Thomas. It was a plant he was fond of. Thus, the small centre bed is divided into a square centre with narrow flanks and so is a prelude to all the beds beyond it.

Planting all the other flower beds, and particularly the square ones, a shape not encountered before, required a new technique. At her drawing board, Marjorie worked out how to create a balance of seasonal representatives in each shape. There was also the need to balance low plants and taller ones. The spread of flowering times had to be as even as possible to avoid gaps until gaps become inevitable as the season passes by.

It was like a game of chess. The pencil ran across the paper and up the paper so often that the drawing began to resemble a chess board. To ensure that each plant would have adequate space to perform at its special moment, she decided to give each plant equal space. Strings were laid in both directions making two-foot-square squares. A large plant might only need one representative planted at the centre, others might require four plants, some sixteen, all evenly spaced to fill their squares.

And what about the height of plants? We had envisaged the creation of a garden-sized meadow, but composed of garden plants and without grass. Heights would be carefully varied and contrasted so that each plant could be seen, and its individuality appreciated, as in a painting by Botticelli. Plants equal in height do not occupy adjacent spaces, and simultaneous flowerers are separated, which ensures that the inevitable spread of gaps after flowering is properly considered and balanced too.

Walking into the flower garden, whether from the house at one end or from the yew hedge at the other, or as for many people through the gate from the car park, there is a rectangular sea of flowers, clearly outlined by a path. You will have to turn one way or another to find a way into the beds by a side path. Twelve beds of flowers are waiting to see you: they are accessible, but pause and see the whole first. It is not at all like a natural wild meadow; it is an artificial dream, different in every respect, a utopian democracy of plants, and it is very organised. The planting of the flowers was completed late in 1980.

The following year the first article presenting and illustrating the garden was published in the RHS magazine, *The Garden*. An unknown writer had called in the grey, still wintery spring to ask our permission. His photographs showed a flat expanse of evenly planted beds with, at that time, very little colour. We had answered his questions and no doubt had spoken of our hopes. But few of the walls were then completed, and shrubs, climbers and hedging plants were very juvenile. His conclusion may have seemed ironic to us, but was an honest appraisal of what he saw; he decided that we had just completed the planting of a large and ambitious new rock garden.

Our visitor was Arthur Hellyer, whose work had been so important to us when our gardening life began at Wallington. Through *Amateur Gardening* he introduced us to Margery Fish, and his book *The Amateur Gardener* solved so many of our problems. He was a very serious man whom we greatly respected. His article brought us visitors for twenty-one years; they may have been progressively surprised by what they saw, for it was not a rock garden. His retired secretary made her pilgrimage in 2007.

His work was addressed to the amateur. Our reading of early gardening history sources confirmed the contributions to the scope and vision of garden-making made century after century by the devotion of amateurs, peasant and professional. The penniless John Clare wrote of the flowers he saw by the cottages, while some vicars studied and recorded wild flowers, and others rescued or bred roses. When the garden speaks to you, you answer the call, 'do your best' and happily join the ranks. The judge puts on his apron, the worker takes up his other tools, the lady cares for the cuttings, and the cornflower is planted at the rectory. The German visitor is astonished to have found flowers on English traffic islands, and I explain that flowers and their necessity may, in part, account for national debt.

Also in 1981, I was invited to contribute a chapter to a garden 'anthology', *The Englishman's Garden*, to be published in 1982. Thirty-three visions of a garden were collected from all corners of England from men of widely differing occupations. Ours was the baby garden, barely even planted, but every garden has a beginning. My suggestion that it might look better if publication was delayed for a year or two was of no avail. Sir David Scott, an important contributor, was already past ninety-five. The words of everyone's essay were strictly limited and counted, and it felt so painful that my contribution lost one sentence. Photographic space equally divided between colour and monochrome was limited too.

It was when I had to confront my own very unsophisticated photographs, in order to write captions for them before publication, that a most important discovery was made about the planting of the flower beds. Describing the largest of the square beds, I simply noted that it was planted 'mainly in shades of pink', That photograph alone seemed pleasing; its unified colour structure made it vibrant. Marjorie had had other reasons for beginning with pink flowers. She had envisaged looking out into the garden from the house, via an architectural frame, into a haze of pink spots with an eruption of colour in the distance. It was a gentle beginning, for she thought of pink as an essentially feminine colour: she had made herself a pink suit for our wedding.

Many of the flowers she chose are still there. She liked 'brush stroke' flowers with small nodding heads, animated by the wind. There are the little persicaria 'bottle brushes', flesh-pink campions with dark centres, scabious, the mist of pink meadowsweet, thin spires of veronicastrum floating dierama, small violas, pink montbretia . . . Par excellence is gypsophila, such as the magnificent ones we had seen at Kew. Sadly it seems that Hartington is a step too far north for their comfort, though little 'Rosy Veil' or 'Veil of Roses' (known to some as 'Rosenschleier') has been a staunch ally.

When the book arrived, it was immediately clear that, apart from that one bed, everything else had to be changed, urgently. 1981 had been the first time that we had seen our flowers since 1975. They certainly looked happy, celebrating their rescue from unavoidable neglect. Our first visitors had enjoyed the show, and some spoke of a 'riot of colour'. Now we knew that, as in all other aspects of life, riots are best avoided. Unless unreasonably inflamed, we are as peaceful as Hartington when untroubled by gales. This may be a passionate garden but it is not an angry one.

However, the complete change needed to be structured. We could now see that colour itself had to be the subject of that garden. The organisation of the shapes had been considered as a composition, and suddenly it was so obvious that we needed to compose in terms of colour too. Pink, cool and pale, could be expanded to follow a course northwards through the warmth of oranges to reach red, to be explored in its richest and darkest forms.

This prospect helped to solve another lingering and hitherto completely independent problem. Early gardens had seemed to need a reference to time; they had needed sundials. We had provided one as a part of the axis, but had then removed its dial. A colour scheme could be invented to make contemporary reference to the haunting and inevitable passage of time, and to allow us the remarkable luxury of experiencing 'morn, noon and (nearly) night' all at once.

The presentation of time in colour had already been achieved in art by the giant figure among the French Impressionists, Claude Monet. His obsession with the structure of light led him to construct series of pictures exploring the same subject matter at different times of day. The image of Rouen Cathedral barely emerges from a misty summer dawn, light and shapes become clearer, it begins to get hot, the shadows are moving, it gets dark . . . At the right moment, each canvas was laid aside, and the next one took its place on the easel. Work continued day by day.

The flower garden has nine flowering beds laid in three stages. We could portray the passage of time through a day. The first three beds could explore the developing sun and the dawn sky; the centre section could luxuriate in the midday sun amid glorious blue skies; and we could see the evening sun with hints of night amid the uncertainties of late skies and clouds.

All the colours are achieved by 'optical mixtures', a sprinkling of colour variations which present different shades together with different hues. Often lighter effects are made by adding a few whites too. Language can seem clumsy. What indeed is pink? Is it 'flesh' or 'salmon' or 'sugar', almost white or deepest rose? Assemble them together and they will vibrate, none more so than the blues. They vary through the season, and they vary with the light. Only the very faintest suggestion of colour might occasionally be glimpsed in the long gap between autumn and spring. What you may see one day will be your memory, on another day you would have seen something else. And since colour itself is so elastic, so variable, and as pink turns towards orange, crimson, mauve or white, who can say if all the colours are in the right place?

The final colour composition provides pink with a pair of cream companions. 'Cream' is achieved by plantings of different yellows with various forms of white. The pivotal centre bed is devoted to orange. Its lighter side is represented by 'apricot' geums and inulas (could this be van Gogh's *Sunflower*?), *Potentilla x tonguei* and small 'peach' tulips. Wallflowers and the lovely small-flowered *Geum chiloense* 'Quellion' offer a tinge of 'brick'; the northern 'John-go-to-bed-at-noon', *Hieracium aurantiacum*, known as 'Fox and Cubs', is spectacular in July with terracotta, gold-centred flowers, while its smaller relative, *Hieracium coccineum*, 'Grim-the-Collier', edges towards vermillion. Various poppies, double and single, contribute, with the double orange Welsh poppy, *Meconopsis cambrica*, very prominent from June. For its darker side, the colour moves towards brown with the *Sedum telephium* 'Atropurpureum', with dark chocolate foliage and milk chocolate flowers. Then there is *Viola* 'Irish Molly', purple four-leaved clover and a few rock roses. Apollo himself appears at the height of summer in the guise of an orange lily, and is carried aloft on a sea of marigolds. On either side are the complementary beds of blue, which contrive to keep the sun shining.

From Eddie's old friend we obtained a pale sky-blue Jacob's ladder, a polemonium which in his honour we still name Gordon Harrison. It is planted with deeper blue forms including *Polemonium cashmerianum,* and there is the violet-blue *Polemonium foliosissimum* too. When different shades coincide there is a shimmer as you walk by. The polemoniums follow early veronicas and from the village came Molly Thompson's gentian, and then, among them, the campanulas begin. It is no surprise that the very local harebells appear, some in extremely pale blue. Surprisingly, they seem able to hybridise with a wonderful small adenophora which was found both in a nearby village and in a garden wall surrounding a neglected one-time farmhouse at Hartington. This has a different leaf, and a rich violet-blue flower as wide as it is deep, the perfect model for a topee hat. If it is not hybridisation, there is a secret competition between the two types to produce the largest bell. The harebells may be winning, for some of their bells are now much larger than wild ones. Then there are tradescantias and salvias. We particularly enjoy the uninhibited extrovert performances of *Salvia pratensis*, the wild meadow sage. Both size of plant and shape vary. Its 'Rosea' form is among the pink flowers, and its 'Alba' variation is in one of the cream beds. July brings geraniums, single and double, pale and stripy, and dark and violet. Tall veronicas appear, and violas cannot be missed, and we begin to know where the season is when the agapanthus starts work. We do grow the old double deep blue one, a gift from James Russell whilst working at Castle Howard, but it is one of the Headbourne hybrids that catches the eye. We tentatively tried it at Wallington when someone told us that it might survive outdoors though no others would. Nothing has inconvenienced it yet.

The red bed has a deep red *Centaurea montana* from a garden near Kendal, the double red *Lychnis coronaria* came from Gretna Green, the red and the black 'black' cranesbills (both are forms of

Geranium phaeum, the Mourning Widow) and the very large deep red poppies sent to us by a kindly German visitor, which can produce four different shades. *Tulipa sprengeri* is wild and noble, everything a tulip should be.

In the enclosing 'pastel' beds we found homes for some of our surviving grey plants. In her last years, Margery Fish was making herself a little not-too-formal 'formal' silver garden. With endless zeal she collected artemesias, centaureas, helichrysums, ballotas, salvias, senecios and santolinas. We still use some of the artemesias and a couple of centaureas, *C. simplicicaulis* and *C. montana* 'Alba'. *Lamium garganicum*, neatly mounded with grey-pink flowers, and a white mauve-edged form of *Iris pumila*, feel at home here, partially edging paths together with carpets of the horned pansies, white and lilac. *Viola cornuta* Lilacina always seems more lavender-blue than lilac, which would perhaps better describe 'pink' forms we have, in two shades, in the pink bed. The Lilacina ones accompany clumps of the native 'lilac' form of *Geranium pyrenaicum* on one side while the white forms of both are together on the other. The corners at the north end have old dusky purple shrub roses, 'Cardinal de Richelieu' and 'Capitaine John Ingram'. Their last grey-pink-mauve petals fall like tears, regretting the passing of summer as we edge into August. A few taller plants are grown with the roses. Their silhouettes, accentuated by the yew hedge, look well from the house. One side has the coarse 'blue', more accurately a greying lavender, form of veronicastrum (the much more refined and floriferous pink and white forms are in the pink bed). The other side answers with the pink form of monkshood (*Aconitum napellus* 'Carneum'). Its dusky spikes, which beckon you if you pause to peer in at the garden gate, could be described as the colour of nostalgia. Along the west side, taller plants are silhouetted by the hollies. The giant *Achillea grandifolia*, with a notable show of flat umbels of creamy white above aromatic green-grey lacy foliage, is beside that perfect mass of mauve-pink bells, *Campanula lactiflora*. Then there is a long-flowering polemonium hybrid of the non-seeding sort, beside *Serratula tinctoria* 'Alba', a knapweed from Kew and a refined form of *Eryngium alpinum*, a silky sea holly without spikes which a local doctor and keen amateur gardener, the late Dr White, gave us long ago. The exquisite loosestrife, *Lysimachia ephemerum*, another grey-green foliage plant with delicate erect spikes of white flowers which first hint at pink, is an especial pleasure.

On the garden gate side, the answering, balancing plants are a little smaller, so that you see through them to their near neighbours across the red bed. There are more cranesbills, including the attractive and modest old 'double white' form of *Geranium pratense*, a favourite Margery Fish phlox, the simple mauve *Phlox paniculata* with widely spaced petals and her 'Lambrook Mauve' Jacob's ladder. (Why did we never find space in our little motor car for her 'Lambrook Pink'?) And there are asters, wild and shaggy. Mrs Pippa Rakusen gave us an unknown old 'bedding' pansy and the white opium poppy she had found in America: treasures from her garden, Ling Beeches near Leeds.

Along the south side, the 'pastel' beds have space for the self-seeders, poppies and wallflowers, and forget-me-nots, here the white ones. The poppies developed by Cedric Morris, the painter and gardener from Benton End in Suffolk, provide all the colours the bed should have, white, dusky mauve, soft pink, while the wallflowers (*Erysimum linofolium*) give their versions of mauve and white. They have the support of wild scabious (*Scabiosa columbaria*), sea lavender, and Siberian irises in white and mauve. If we cannot define 'pink', 'mauve' would be no smaller task.

And so space was found for some of the tall plants we had collected. But fearing for their safety, particularly at the north, yew hedge end of the garden, where the swooping wind headed for the yew arch over the garden gate, Marjorie decided to plant an internal box hedge to protect the red bed and support the taller silhouettes in the pastel beds. This was duly planted along the inner side of the surrounding border and continued along the short entry paths.

Now three feet high, the hedge creates a sense of mystery by concealing all but the heads of the taller plants. They show as red and purple spots, but what else is there inside this miniature Roman camp? To complete its secret, cubes of box were planted in the red bed to obscure any view from along the short central paths. The sundial stands in the centre, midway between the cubes.

It was always intended to include topiary in the flower garden. There is topiary in all the other gardens. The new internal box hedge contributes a sense of enclosure to the upper end of the flower garden which contrasts particularly with the central orange and blue section. Blue is always described as a spatial colour and these beds seem to float. The pastel beds were further enclosed by miniature towers with rounded tops. Or perhaps they are pepper pots. These are placed at the four outer corners, and there are two more guarding the north entrance to the red bed from the yew hedge. They are not repeated on the other side where the flow of poppies is not interrupted.

Only the orange bed, the smallest bed, has no topiary, though it may have the oldest and finest of the troughs. This exactly resembles a small group of fonts found in Herefordshire which were discussed in *Country Life* some years ago, while its relief carving is the same as that on the Saxon cresset in Hexham Abbey. Our 'Apollo' (*Lilium bulbiferum* var. *croceum*) stands guard, and birds drink and sometimes bathe in its often less than pure water.

The blue beds each have box spirals placed at their centres. They are larger than the pepper pots, and are not a pair. Just as the plants in the twin beds do not repeat themselves, the spirals too have a life of their own. Spirals are dynamic, they are busy going somewhere, and seem to fit with the spatial restless character of blue itself.

But just at the edge of each blue bed, by the path which separates them from their cream neighbours, you will sense that you are getting closer to the house and the kitchen. Each has a small conical 'cake' of Korean box with tiny leaves. Mothers kept everyone going with what are sometimes called 'cup' cakes.

These are matched on the other side of the path, as you might expect, by a pair of 'cottage loaves', much larger and oval-shaped. There are made from another, larger-leaved form of Korean box; their colour is a lighter green than hedging box.

The pink bed has two pairs of topiaries. Two globes of 'tree box' come first and then, in white variegated hedging box, the sequence ends in a pair of 'teapots'. Marjorie had wanted a pair of her favourite blackbirds on cylindrical plinths, but that did not happen. We keep a white china teapot of similar form to the garden ones in the pantry. The major difference is a question of function; the pantry one has both a handle and a spout, neither of which is required in the garden. With topiaries, it may be better not to reveal the source of inspiration; and it may have been wise to avoid blackbirds. I once explained to an admiring visitor to the garden that the pair of tall clipped cylinders of green Irish yew, now close by, growing out of their cushions of Miss Jekyll's periwinkle, are our 'Pillars of Wisdom.' 'But,' he replied, 'should there not be seven Pillars of Wisdom?' Clearly we still lack some of the virtues.

For the 'pepper pots', gold variegated hedging box was used and the white variegated 'Elegantissima' form was used in the short section of hedge from the red bed to the yew hedge.

Replanting the flower garden has been a success. We have no memories of doing extra work, for working with conviction is entirely joyful. Giving the colours space to express themselves removed the conflicts and confusions. There are echoes of other colours everywhere just as you will find them in paintings, but the main theme is stated and variations can be enjoyed without losing sight of the structure. The variations might tease you, but teasing is a gentle form of humour.

The deliberate varying of height in adjacent plants – putting low ones beside tall ones – is also doubly significant. It gives the flower garden a textural quality, which in itself is a meadow-like feature, and it further distances Marjorie's planting style from that of Gertrude Jekyll, who so carefully graded both heights and colours so that each element was skilfully blended into the next, allowing her to create a two-dimensional pictorial effect. Marjorie's garden is three-dimensional. It is designed so that you can enter into her picture to experience both its organisation and its floral content.

Marjorie's monumental job in creating her planting plans in 1988, some six years after the replanting, records her choices with great precision. Some plants have now disappeared. Occasionally, we have recovered and reinstated a lost treasure, and we still find great pleasure in a new face which fits in. But we regret some losses, for to gardeners, plants are members of your intimate family.

Looking down on to the garden from upstairs, you can still identify the 'chess board' though edges and dividing lines have melted away. Throughout the planting Marjorie cherished and used annuals and biennials whose capacity to seed keeps the garden alive. Birds and wind contribute variations to your order you would not imagine. A gardener's restraining hand may be required and sometimes the gardener will be enchanted. We will not have red poppies among Cedric Morris's pastel ones nor will pastel ones in turn find a home among the red ones. In a well-trained garden the plants just know where home is, or so we may tell you.

When first planted, it may possibly have looked as if Marjorie had created a garden version of Paul Klee's famous series of 'magic square' watercolours. These mysterious works explore the magic of colour interactions without reference to external subject matter, within a structure of even squares. But this was not so. Her planting method arose purely from her practical gardener's response to the challenge of achieving within the simple shape a balanced distribution of plants of all sizes, representing all seasons, so that all could be individually seen and appreciated.

Above: the 'riot' of colour exploding after the initial planting (1980).
Opposite: Marjorie's coloured sketch plan of the organised colour scheme which followed.

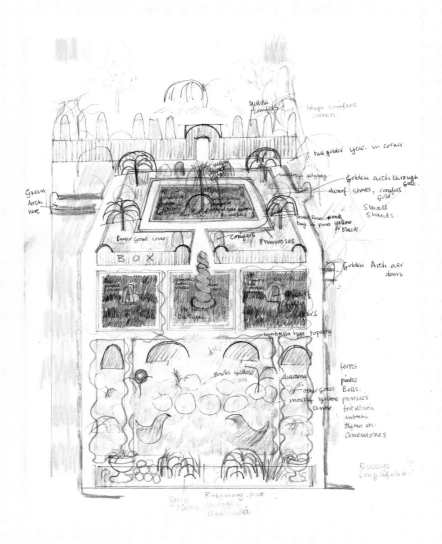

Above: the flower garden in July and the surrounding landscape: 'the garden within the lawn'.

Opposite: 1. *Doronicum*, 'Miss Mason' 2. *Silene dioica* 'Flore Pleno' (double red campion) 3. *Lamium galeobdolon* 'Variegatum' 4. *Centaurea montana* red form (red cornflower) 5. *Paeonia mlokosewitschii* (seed-head) 6. *Ranunculus acris* 'Flore Pleno' (bachelor's buttons) 7. *Eryngium alpinum* 8. *Ranunculus bulbosus* 'Speciosus Plenus' 9. *Colchicum* 'Lilac Wonder'.

Opposite: the sundial in the red bed masked by the Chinese red burnet, *Sanguisorba sitchensis*.
Above: *Salvia pratensis* and forms of polemonium surround one of the box spirals. An
unknown locally found adenophora is in the left corner.

Some of the orange flowers with violet-blue *Polemonium foliosissimum* in the foreground. A Saxon pot is at the centre.

A detail of the golden border frame. Ivy 'Buttercup' covers a stone mortar below the holly 'Golden King'. *Molinia caerulea* subsp. *arundinacea* 'variegata' is the grass in the foreground.

Above: two different gold variegated saxifrages: the tiny pale pink
S. cuneifolia in the raised trough above a carpet of *S. umbrosa*
(London Pride).
Opposite: the entrance to the flower garden below the golden yew
arch; the not quite pink *Aconitum napellus* 'Carneum' is in the centre.

THE FORMAL, THE PHYSIC AND THE FANCY

The flower garden is much the largest of the four decorative parts of the garden. If you have seen it in high summer, it may be the part you recall first, should you describe the garden to someone else. Like that garden, the designs of both the formal and physic gardens also differ from the 1975 drawing and both, in like manner, found their actual design on the ground in direct response to the buildings they were attached to. The fourth garden, the 'fancy' garden, is, as originally intended, devoted to pattern but did not find its present form for twenty years. The site was carefully laid out and prepared, but quite quickly the concept which had shaped it was recognised as a failure and abandoned. The space found other temporary use.

The Formal

The formal garden between the house and the lane meets the landscape and presents us to the world. Jimmy's low front wall directly matches the low seventeenth-century listed wall on the other side of the lane. This is actually a taller retaining wall supporting the road verge, and may be ancient terracing to support the 'modern' old lane.

The two walls make a pair, though you might think that ours, which is so densely covered in ivy, is an ivy hedge. Its modesty has a purpose; it offers visual access for the traveller to both garden and house. It is gesture of respectful hospitality. The formal garden itself is a similar tribute; we are formally dressed for the occasion, we have put on a suit for the meeting. The hedge tops are trimmed and square, perhaps reminiscent of a well-ironed shirt collar. Margery Fish's book, *Cottage Garden Flowers*, describes her plant-hunting expeditions in rural Somerset. Visual access to gardens for her served a different purpose, since she was plant-hunting!

Beyond the field wall, the landscape is flamboyantly informal. The meadow's edges beside the river are damp where the river can swell and rise far above its edges after prolonged heavy rain. On its banks waves of rushes rise and fall in the wind, and waves of flowers follow lost channels which drained water from the copse. July is bright with yellow iris, then pink with masses of wild valerian, and cream with meadowsweet and angelica. A little further away is a mad scramble of blackberries.

The landscape beyond the garden is not hospitable, but it provides an encyclopaedic interpretation of green. It possesses prolific energy. While we grow a modest 'bee-skep' in a yellow box, it can raise four new alders from small balls to perfectly formed twenty footers. Sitting at the table, I might imagine taking shears to their edges, but could not and would not; my edges are smooth, theirs are rough. It is stimulating to see our different orders together. And we can wonder at Capability Brown, walking across these meadows to school in the village, dreaming of turning the great Northumbrian lawn into the classical English landscape garden.

Marjorie planted the verge on the other side of the road to make a bridge to the landscape beyond the garden. Five clumps of wild ferns were set at very irregular intervals, and the spaces between them filled with woodrushes. However, these are not quite the same as those which carpet Wallington woods, but Margery Fish's form, which, on close inspection, will be found to have a fine edge of creamy white. It is variegated. The turf in front is a very organic mix of grasses, mosses and wild things. It has only a superficial relationship to a gardener's lawn.

The formal garden is L-shaped. The main square section, which is almost the width of the house, slopes down to the road. But the low front wall then turns back to enclose a car park for house callers. At the back of this it is heightened and becomes a retaining wall for the further narrow section. It is high enough to form, on the garden side, a long low bench where you can sit for a moment and take a view over the whole little garden.

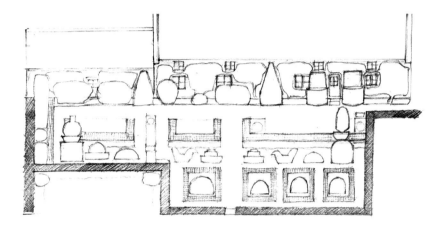

The second section, in front of the bothy door, was once a little vegetable patch and its soil is higher. This is protected by a low retaining wall pierced by a single step. The wall was made wide enough to form two narrow flower beds.

Parallel to the low front wall, Marjorie planted a box hedge now three feet high, and almost as wide, across the entire garden, twelve feet in front of the house. It is cut into three sections by the main broad entrance path from the low front gate, and two further narrow paths either side of the low retaining beds. The hedge and the walls make a powerful frame for the garden in between them. This has a strong geometric flavour; it is full of squares, right angles and circular topiaries.

Just inside the front wall there are four rectangular box enclosures, perhaps reflecting the four small upper windows of the house. They are a foot high, and almost as wide, and are reminiscent of shallow boxes. Inside them are four 'bee-skeps' in brilliant yellow Japanese box. Splashes of yellow may be the first indication for the traveller that there is a garden ahead. On closer inspection, they have a fringe of pale pink dicentra in front and behind them.

The traveller will also notice two high topiaries in yew growing from each end of a line of topiaries, behind the bee-skeps, which stretches right across the garden. The eastern landmark is the 'fountain', a 'gushing' cone above a basin, above a wider 'bubbling' base. The base initially had two graded sections, but the judgement of time rules in favour of monumental simplicity. The 'crown' represents the western extremity.

Should you begin your topiaries with clear thoughts and plans, and train them with canes, string and wires, or perhaps let them evolve in line with thoughts and observations, with general compositional ideas of having something tall here and something short there? What would the pioneer gardeners who first set such magnificent gardens as Levens think of the immense and wonderful forms now present? Did they foresee the forms, or would they have dreamt of different things expressing cultural values as remote from ours as they themselves now are from us?

Whatever approach you take, time to see and to think is important. The simple composition of two tall forms framing seven smaller ones has seemed appropriate to the simple elongated shape of the garden. Supports were used in two of the small topiaries, while the form of the tall yews has been achieved after many rethinks and re-evaluations.

The 'fountain' once had a wide and elaborate basin, but the wider it became, the more difficult it was to reach the top section. The proportions of the different sections were stretched and uncomfortable. It was duly simplified. But the evolution of the 'crown' was much more painful. Its ambition had been to become a peacock, a memory of the remarkable village bird not so far away. Its dramatic silhouette would have announced the garden splendidly, its tail perhaps spreading down over the retaining wall into the car park while its fine head gazed towards the house. Unfortunately, this required a south–north alignment. The tail grew happily towards the south, but the head and shoulders, which looked north into gloom, made no progress. In this brief season, light is everything. Had the axis been east–west, the bird might have prospered, but its impact would have been lost. After twenty-two years of explaining the odd headless phenomenon to all who enquired, I then, with glee, cut off the tail. The fat rounded body got a new life, its shape enhanced by a great cubic base.

Two of the low forms were taller until two successive winters of heavy snow thoroughly damaged their upper parts and a new formal modesty was accepted. Five are circular; two are domes, one a dome above a dome, and two are cylindrical with stepped sides and formerly supported spheres. The remaining are a pair of speckled hens in white variegated box, and these were prepared initially with the help of canes.

The eighteenth-century poets, who prepared the progress of the landscape garden by making fun of the now unimaginably ambitious and complex creations of their contemporary topiarists, still haunt us. Attention, but not sympathy, was drawn to the case of a goddess badly affected by a recent gale during which her arm became detached or, far worse, it may have been her noble head. The poets' painful stabs were deeply inserted. Here, if any detail is put in the path of rising wind, or an important edge subjected to prolonged frost or drought, your work may suffer. And hens, which unavoidably possess such details, are also subject to visitors' very subjective interpretations, as are the teapots. In a small windy country garden, geometric simplicity is to be recommended.

As a focal point between the vertical yews, Marjorie planted a third green yew against the house, at its centre. It might have become another buttress, but instead became the 'needle'. From a rectangular base, five feet wide, three deep and three high, it rises as a pyramid tapering almost to a point from both the sides and the front, stopping just below the slates. Looking into the garden from the gate, the three tall yews appear to be roughly equally spaced and tied together by the long box hedge.

Behind the topiaries and in front of the box hedge, there is an equally long narrow flower border. Its front edge has a ribbon of a lemon-yellow, citrus-smelling, non-flowering thyme (*Thymus pulegioides*

'Aureus') planted from end to end. Its luminous colour is a pleasure in all seasons. Even in winter, should your foot brush its foliage, you will enjoy the lovely smell.

At each end, Marjorie planted huge clumps of white variegated day lily, *Hemerocallis fulva* 'Kwanso Variegata'. It produces some pale apricot trumpets in August, but in this foliage garden it is the mass of boldly striped leaves that is striking. The central short length of border, approaching the retaining wall, is 'stopped' by another hemerocallis, the green-leaved old double form of *H. fulva* called simply 'Kwanso'. In this more central position, its large warm orange flowers with brick-red centres are welcome in late summer.

The other flowers follow the seasons, beginning with thousands of *Crocus tommasinianus* with seedlings now in many variations of the lilac type, spread from end to end. Then this is the garden for the crown imperials, yellow at one end, red at the other, with the best a fine orange in the centre section, which came from Sir Stephen Middleton's old border at Bitchfield, the dower house of Belsay Hall.

There is the old yellow 'cottage' lily, *Lilium pyrenaicum*, from a garden in Coquetdale, whose odd but distinctive smell marks a stage of the advance of the season, and the yellow asphodel, *Asphodeline lutea*. Its narrow 'lily' flowers open haphazardly every evening during the early months, well above its distinctive blue-grey leaves. Summer brings white valerian, *Centranthus ruber* 'Albus', and the white mulleins, *Verbascum chaixii* 'Album', and creamy white foxgloves. Either side of the main path there are large clumps of sea hollies, the variegated form of *Eryngium planum* on the left and *Eryngium variifolium* on the right. They provide welcome blue flowers for August and beyond. Sadly, Miss Thompson's madonna lilies did not settle in, but the galtonias offer their white bells without fail later. At Kew we had particularly admired the bold round white flower heads of *Silene compacta* and were thrilled to obtain some seed. Plants of this biennial appear as freely as the crocuses, but for over thirty years we have never had a white one. Without exception our flowers are a gentle shade of cerise, which we now look forward to. It is a very happy partnership, never anticipated, with the lemon-yellow foliage of the thyme.

From the road, you might assume that the garden you see in front of the box hedge is the garden, but the hedge turns back for a further yard beside the paths, and these 'returns' enclose narrow beds on the north side of the hedge in the central and far western sections. In the other part, in front of the front door, there is stone paving with enough space for a small group of carol singers, should any be passing.

On either side of the path which runs from the paving to the far end of the garden there is a second narrow 'secret' garden. On the shaded side of the hedge Marjorie planted fine 'garden' ferns in contrast to the wild ones along the road verge. Two are memories from Wallington, Edith Bulmer's *Polystichum setiferum* and Mrs Masson's crested lady fern (*Athyrium filix-femina* 'Vernoniae Cristatum'), which had a place in her 'best' front courtyard garden. There are eight specimens altogether, but they have been found and collected here and there so that it would need a fern collector to name them. My mother Evie's younger sister Janet loved ferns, and wherever she lived she managed to contrive a space for them beside her house, not far from the door. She always gave us what we liked, and Marjorie planted her shuttlecock fern under the Victorian windows we later added to the north side of the house. Their great height and bold form seem very comfortable with the scale of the Victorian stone frames, and their bright green spring fronds are a fine contrast to the mounds of purple *Viola labradorica* which surround them.

The house walls required some flowers for late spring and early summer, for that period just before flowers have generally appeared. Marjorie chose *Lonicera caprifolium*, the goat-leaf honeysuckle, allegedly grown in English gardens for half a millennium. The delightfully scented flowers are here for May Day and last well into June. Its rather bluish leaves have the distinctive habit of providing a saucer for each flower to sit on, as the two uppermost leaves join together, making a dignified support. It is a parent of *Lonicera x americana,* which inherited the same habit. Marjorie planted that one on the front of the granary.

Clematis montana var. *alba* makes the greatest contribution; two forms are used. The stronger and more prolific one has quite small flowers which come a little later, but they possess the most memorable vanilla-like smell. This is *Clematis montana* var. *wilsonii*. The early twentieth-century plant-hunter, E.H. 'Chinese'

Wilson, did a great service by discovering and introducing this to our gardens. On warm evenings, when the small upstairs windows will be open until light has gone, the house fills with warm scent.

After this, you are close to the front door, and for this last section ivies are used. To the left of the door, the curly leaved *Hedera helix* 'Green Ripple', overhung with clematis, begins. Marjorie put a thin frame of the shy yellow *H. h.* 'Buttercup' around the door, and completed the wall with another green form whose new leaves are a bright lime, almost lemon. After the wall has been closely clipped, sometime in August, the response can be startling.

The narrow house border manages to support a lot of growth, as at Anne Hathaway's. Two tall box plants suggest a porch at the door. They are in two parts; the taller upper section is rectangular but their bases are wider and jut out to a curved front. The upper windows are close to the floor and leave no space to attempt to grow a porch roof.

To the left of the needle is a wide clipped flowering ivy shrub which does not form a sphere here as we saw it doing at Stratford. Our sphere is of yellow variegated hedging box and comes next, but some think that with hens around it may be an egg. In either case it is a little flattened by its proximity to the house wall. Then another green yew marks the east end of the low byre. This repeats the form of the needle but is truncated to conform to the lower roof. In a small space on its right is a tiny shrub of white variegated ivy. Its progress is very slow. It was propagated in 1968 from a cutting taken from its climbing form after this had been removed, as part of the formal replanting strategy, from the front of the house at Wallington.

The last section of planting, either side of the bothy door, is of yellow variegated snowberry, *Symphoricarpus orbiculatus*. This species does not produce suckers and if it ever flowered, which it never has, would produce pink berries. The wall behind them has jasmines, winter on the left and, on the right, a gold variegated form of the summer one, which came from the front of Hauxley Hall, near Amble. Marjorie put a gold variegated form of the winter jasmine in the flower garden.

Planting was completed at the west end with a deeper shelter bed of box, holly and yew. At the south corner, behind the crown, is the low 'thatched cottage' of yellow variegated box. In the centre is a tall cone of an old green Scottish holly, with small dark distinctly curled leaves without prickles, named in the 1980s by a holly expert from Kew as *Ilex contorta*. For the north corner we planted the very largest and widest of Matheson's golden yews. It is now twelve feet across and twelve high with a gently curved top.

The border is edged with a three-foot hedge of sarcococca, corresponding with the base of the holly cone. The yew's clipped rectangular form overhangs the hedge, appearing to jut forward like a medieval house front. The cottage, too, rests its roof on the same support.

Working in that garden after Christmas is rewarded by wafts of scent from the tiny hidden cream sarcococca flowers. February brings the crocuses and the ivy berries, and just a little sunshine excites the winter irises, *Iris unguicularis*. These live beside and even on the great field boulders on which the old house rests. With their backs to the wall, set between the 'egg' and the ivy, the large slightly scented lavender flowers can be tempted to appear by any nod or wink from the sun from December till the end of April. For them, it must awaken very dim memories of having once lived in Algeria. They are a target for wild bees seeking their first pollen of the year.

The Physic

Jimmy's task in the physic garden was to complete the southern boundary wall by filling in the gap through which the cows had walked into the little yard, on their way to be milked in the stalls behind the granary arches. After the ground had been prepared for planting, Arthur added a new eastern wall continuing past the garden to enclose the adjacent materials yard. It is pierced by a narrow gate for communication.

A wide path was made in front of the arches with planting pockets of deep soil left for climbers. Then the usual width main paths were made at the east side, in line with the corner of the granary, and along the south side. This made a rectangular central plot with a sheltering east border, split by a path leading to the yard, and a very deep south border with space for both shelter shrubs and herbaceous plants.

In the east border, Marjorie planted tree box each side of the path, and two forms of *Rosa alba*. Marjorie's Uncle Norman had given us the very pure double white, and from Mrs Masson we got the 'Maiden's Blush'. Whatever someone says to a maiden to produce such a beautiful blush is quickly forgiven for it soon fades to a perfect pale pink complexion. Old writers speculated whether England was called 'Albion' because of the white cliffs of Dover or because of its abundance of *Rosa alba*. It seemed essential to plant these old treasures first.

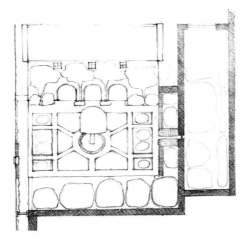

The south-east corner is dominated by a now huge blue juniper, *Juniperus squamata* 'Meyeri'. Once you have rubbed its foliage and experienced its curiously pungent smell, instinctively you will want to do so again. The wild juniper, associated with gin drinking, must once have lived here. Long ago, early writers talked of the great Border juniper forest. Tiny specimens survive in high wild places; we found them when picnicking on beautifully grazed turf among the heather in the great wilderness where Weardale meets Teesdale. Stumpy little green bushes were everywhere around us. Clearly, sheep enjoy juniper without gin.

Next along the south wall, Marjorie planted the white variegated philadelphus, then lilacs, a locally found single red and a very fine double white, the prolific six-month flowering *Viburnum x bodnantense*, and finally *Hamamelis mollis*, the witch hazel. Its mass of yellow flowers is a winter delight, always catching sunlight or making it. Its smell is as elusive as the violet's, but should you despair that you have lost that vital sense, just try the viburnum beside it, or walk round the corner of the house and find the sarcococca.

The therapeutic value of smell made it a necessity for the physic garden. A well-scented sprig, like a summer posy, could be put into a jug and taken indoors to raise fallen spirits, to 'touch the soul', to bring joy to the sad. How strange are the English, a German traveller in the first Elizabethan era mused in his diary, with their little jugs of flowers in their houses. It is sensible not to plant scented things in our traffic islands. Smell has not lost its hypnotic magic.

Flowers and scent were the characteristics most required of the climbers which enclose this, the tiniest of the gardens. Honeysuckles were chosen, *Lonicera x heckrottii* for the west barn wall, early and late 'Dutch' at either end of the granary, with *L. americana*, sometimes home to the flycatchers, at the base of the two central arch piers. The scent of the eglantine travels far on a summer evening, and if it combines with that of elderflowers, it makes a heady country cocktail. We once tasted our good friend Mary Cookson's elderflower sorbet which must have come directly from heaven.

At the feet of the Dutch honeysuckles, Marjorie planted our favourite double lilac form of Scots Burnet rose, *Rosa pimpinellifolia*. We got this from the late Mary McMurtrie of Balbithan House near Kintore, Aberdeenshire, when we made our pilgrimage to see Pitmedden and Crathes. To see a Scottish hedge with six or more different coloured forms in full flower could be like witnessing a medieval army on the march with flags and banners flying. One was planted in the garden of the 'old house' in the centre of Haddington designed by Sir George Taylor for the Lamp of Lothian Trust. There may have been a hundred or more cultivars by the end of the Georgian period, but then they were widely abandoned because of their disgraceful spreading habits. New roses were bred which took their places.

Ours are contained by the compacted stone paths. Otherwise you need a sharp spade in the spring to remove runners. One summer evening we made one of our occasional pilgrimages to look with awe at the work of 'Mr Tidy' of Whittingham. The work of this retired widower had made him into a legend. It was there that I learnt about ivy clipping. Before he retired he had been a gardener, and now he did nothing else. He was always busy. He might be just on the other side of his long and perfectly kept hedge, or he might appear from under the bridge pushing his large wooden wheelbarrow.

His cottage garden sloped down to the river. Outside on the river bank, he had made a small group of topiaries. Looking down from the river bridge, I noticed a pink rose oddly protruding from the top of a neat cone of glaucous foliage. Was this sabotage? He was always rightly too busy for idle conversation, but there he was. I had to ask how that flower came to be there. 'Well, it is a rose,' he said, and that was that. Only he might have tamed and trained such wild exuberance.

He was not a philosopher, he kept everything neat and tidy, grew only what he liked, and grew it well. Everything was set in perfect rows across the garden, one plant only per row. His line of the rare and so desirable black veratrums was followed by a line of excellent pointed cabbages. After we had gone, did he cut that flower off?

As elsewhere, the design of the central area was worked out with strings in front of the granary. A large square was made out of the rectangle, exactly reflecting the width across the arches. After the usual narrow paths were added, space remained for a pair of narrow side beds. These were cut into three parts, making a pair of small square beds with a rectangular one between.

The planting policy for these was to put bitter and sweet things together. Each of the four square corner beds received an aromatic bitter herb, wormwood or 'old woman' on the north side, southernwood or 'old man' on the south. The two wormwoods are the wild grey herb *Artemesia absinthium* and Margery Fish's brighter 'Lambrook Silver' form. The southernwoods are the common form of *Artemisia abrotanum* and its less common camphor-scented form.

The longer central beds each received a pair of 'sweet' sixteenth-century roses, the old 'black' 'Tuscany' on the north side and the light, bright *Rosa mundi (R. gallica* 'Versicolor'*)* on the south.

Bitters may once have been as commonly used as the sweet herbs. They may have been used in country beers and for medicinal purposes, but they were also taken at 'bitter' times, such as Passover, or when memory demanded due respect be paid to personal tragedies or other sad occasions. Rose petals were made into sweet confections, rosewater produced in the still rooms. Roses with many petals were more valuable in this context than the old singles, but the singles provided the rosehip syrup which was so valuable for the children during the war.

Old Dick from Westmorland called every summer and always stooped to gather a few tiny leaves of southernwood. He chewed them as his father and his grandfather had done. He was near to ninety-nine when he died. But why did the Scots call southernwood 'apple-ringy'? All knew the name but couldn't explain until one day a quietly spoken elderly lady told me that it might be because in the old days if you had an apple tree you would plant a ring of southernwood around it. Whatever pests and 'bugs' they were host to got on very badly with those who preyed on apple trees. They went to war with each other, to the great benefit of your precious apple tree. (It is possible that the very distinctive smell of southernwood may have been a deterrent factor too.)

Exactly in line with the centre arch, a circular bed was made at the centre of the square. This is easily inscribed in the ground in schoolboy fashion. Drive in a centre stake, tie on to it a long string and, at the chosen radius, tie on a bamboo cane. Walk around once or twice carefully drawing your outline. However, to then insert a ring of raised edging stones upon the circle proved to be our greatest feat of engineering.

Levelling sites meant effectively controlling the slope of the land and had nothing to do with spirit levels. Those were reserved for much later, for the tops of hedges. Here the ground gently inclines from side to side and top to bottom. Stones were selected to make the raised edge for this prominent feature of the raised circular bed within a square. Strings set at the height of a stone were tied tightly across from opposite corners of the square and from the centres of each side. Where these crossed the incised circle, Bob laid the first stones perfectly. However, to fill the spaces in between proved to be impossible. I stood well back and Bob improvised, but viewed from a distance whatever he did seemed to either rise above the soil or to sink into it. It was clear that more and more strings were required, crossing from carefully measured points on all sides of the square. Eventually the site must have resembled an Islamic ceiling. As soon as all were in place, Bob was able to place and lay each stone perfectly. It is now just a stone circle in tune with the earth it stands on, filled with a centrally raised mound of soil covered in clipped periwinkle below a central topiarised pear tree: but for those who know and care, it has a secret history.

With squares and rectangles to the side, a circle in the centre, the design of the remaining space had to be resolved. After working in front of the arches, the initial sight of which had determined the function of the garden, it was time to pay direct homage to them. Arch shapes, stretching from the centre of the top edge of the square to each corner except for a narrow central entry path, were incised with a cane in the soil. The shapes looked clumsy, a confusion of curves. And so as token arches, simple pentagons were created from the top and bottom edges and that was the solution. The remaining side spaces became pentagons too.

The weeping silver pear tree is now one of the garden's largest topiaries and the only one which needs to be cut twice, in early July and early October. Its shape is well explained in Marjorie's plan drawing. She made it appear to have simply leapt forward out of the central arch. It is a ghostly grey, three-dimensional arch.

It is also at the centre of a central axis across the garden which links the door into the garden visitor's room at the centre of the barn through the pear to the path to the materials yard. This is now expressed through three living three-dimensional arches. Around the door is a very large Romanesque one in ivy. It has been grown in the miniature ivy, *Hedera helix* 'Minima' *(Hedera h.* 'Spetchley'), and has taken over thirty years to form. The top edge has at last joined and was cut for the first time in 2013. At the opposite side, the tree box has formed the third square-faced 'arch', split through the centre in Henry Moore style to accommodate the path.

Graham Thomas described Marjorie's planting of the six beds around the pear as 'posy' style. His words instantly sounded perfectly apt. Plants of contrasting sizes with different smells and purposes thrust their flowers in front of you as the seasons pass.

All the beds have edgings like dressmakers' seams and joiners' chamfers. Early books listed many possibilities for the making of knot gardens. Francis Bacon mentioned thyme. Both prostrate and bushy forms can be wonderfully scented. The flat-growing Corsican *Thymus herba-barona*, to add flavour to your barons of beef, is remarkably powerful, and both the bush forms of common and lemon thyme are powerful too. But here, the bushy ones become winter weary. They may atone for shedding most of their stems by producing a few new ones in the early summer, but they are too untidy for edging. Even so, choice was wide for large or small beds, including lavender, cotton lavender and germander. Marjorie chose germander to put in front of the two forms of *Rosa alba*, white-flowered thrift around the little side beds, and the miniature form of London Pride around the pentagons. Edgings are a formal courtesy and do not have to be eaten.

The physic garden represents a possible version of the farmer's wife's cabinet of curiosities. It includes her medicine chest and other economic necessities. There are a few pot herbs and table delicacies. There are dye plants, poisons, 'strewing' herbs and glue.

The farmer's wife was also the district nurse. Her knowledge was distilled from the thoughts and memories of past generations, and probably rooted in the medieval doctrine of signatures. This alleged that every plant was designed for the benefit of man, but their use was only revealed by man's eye and wit. Each specimen carried a coded message or secret instruction but this had to be discovered. The system supported experiment and chance and was full of danger. However, should a remedy fail and even precipitate disaster, only thankfulness and praise were due for help received. Death could be caused as easily by evil thought as by poison. Defence against evil thoughts and spirits during the night vigil could be secured by planting an elderberry in a prominent position on the edge of your ground. The Scots had equal faith in the rowan or mountain ash. Perhaps in view of our proximity to the border, Marjorie planted both.

A few old sayings are most expressive. 'How can a man die who grows sage in his garden?' The Elizabethans are said to have preferred the purple-leaved form, and I wonder if this gave a pink tinge to one of their mysterious delights, sage creams? Sage tea is good for you. A few leaves in a china teapot with boiling water make a gentle pale green afternoon refreshment. It also has the curious effect of seeming to be cleaning your teeth at the same time. Roman soldiers are said to have rubbed their teeth with sage leaves.

And if only 'they would take the nettle in March, and the mugwort in May, they would have far fewer maidens to lay in the clay.' Nettle tea requires a handful of young leaves in early spring – they are of no use later when they are thinking of flowering – boiled in a pint of water, simmered and bottled. Take a wine glass morning and night. It is a blood tonic and will get you up in the morning. Mugwort, *Artemesia vulgaris*, flowers in July in the north, and it was the flowering tops that were probably used. We grow Margery Fish's white variegated form.

Lesser celandine was called pilewort and here you will find a refined white-flowered form. Greater celandine, *Chelidonium majus*, is in the cut-leaved, cut-petalled form. All its parts are full of natural iodine to relieve your midge bites. But while you may obtain relief, you will also be tattooed by its yellow stain for a few days. Motherwort (*Leonurus cardiaca*) was a valued bee plant but was also used in the prevention of motherhood. Comfrey (*Symphytum officinale*) was 'knit-bone', used for swollen joints and sprains, and also highly regarded for providing comfrey fritters. A succulent leaf cooked in batter was especially tasty. We have plenty of 'gout-weed', also known as 'bishop-weed', a white variegated form of *Aegopodium podagraria*. This is a dangerous spreader, commonly called 'ground elder', Here it is contained by a partly sunken double vertical wall of stout plastic, twelve inches deep. Local marjoram could improve many dishes, chives too. You could try the purple-flowered salsify (*Tragopogon porrifolius*) or a root of skirret (*Sium sisarum*), or take some land cress. But what was done with spignel (*Meum athamaticum*) – such a pretty aromatic herb of the parsley family? It has a lovely English name. Borage here is the small perennial form with turquoise flowers (*Borago laxiflora*). As with the common taller annual form, if you peel off the hairy outer skin of a stem, inside you will find a thin 'stick' of translucent green which will taste better than cucumber.

The Morpeth botanist, William Turner, in his *A New Herbal*, relates that schoolboys used bluebell bulb glue in the manufacture of their exercise books. Camomile and agrimony made teas. Marjorie recalls hearing of Mr Shade, whose garden around a nearby cottage was entirely devoted to camomile. Everyone would knock at his back door for a little medicine at the time of coughs and sneezes.

Meadowsweet had its uses: it is reported to have been Queen Elizabeth's favourite strewing herb for her chambers, and she like it mixed with water mint. Did the good men go out to mow the meadows at dawn in order to deliver fresh supplies in time for breakfast at 6 a.m.?

The little garden reminds us of how much we have forgotten, some of which we knew not so long ago. But the plants remain ever fresh and sinister, and ever dangerous.

The old herbals offer many suggested uses but no precise instructions. Apothecaries understood the language, and read hidden implications. However, I was very pleased to discover what might be done with 'clary' from a small party of members of the American Herb Society. 'Clary' means 'clear-eye' and is *Salvia sclarea* var. *turkestanica*. It is an imposing, handsome biennial whose large, textured leaves develop a pungent, not altogether pleasant smell. Take a few seeds and place them in a saucer of water; they will dissolve and that is your liquid. It was long after the visitors had left that I began to wonder about quantities and, particularly, about application.

For the weavers' dyes we offer weld, *Reseda luteola*, for yellow and alkanet, *Pentaglottis sempervirens*, for red. Woad was judged too invasive a seeder for this garden. Eleanour Sinclair Rohde gave us some lovely Saxon names for plants. In her various books you will find 'joy of the ground' (periwinkle) and 'way-broad' (plantain). We grow the sixteenth-century 'green rose' plantain which Gerard rightly described as 'a curious plant for curious people', 'curious' then implying those who possessed intellectual curiosity.

Under the arches two old settles offer repose. They escape rain and snow but endure the air and the winds. Like the dry-stone walls they have acquired a silvery, grey skin which itself is restful. Behind them is a deep border once intended for ferns, which found it too dark. Wild ivies were planted instead and they make an exuberant edge to the stone paving below the seats. Their foliage, growing towards the light, rises and falls back like the sea meeting the beach.

Among the ivies, the Viking and the Falconer stare out over the settles to the garden. These ancient figures were once a part of the magnificent collection which defiantly confronts the world from the battlements of Alnwick Castle. Did they frighten the bold Scots as schoolboys once believed? Like other escapees, once not uncommon in Northumbrian gardens, ours have each lost an arm, which may once have brandished a sword. We have seen others which had fared worse and lost a leg or legs or, worst of all, their head. It is said that such wounded warriors were retired long ago by dukes to the safe keeping of the town's freemen. From their possession, they travelled further. These were bought in Scotland together with the 'tri-faceted' (three-faced) Scottish sundial, a 'Bonnie Dundee', who perches above the centre arch. The figures had once belonged to the town's convent garden. Sir Paul Getty found five more and had a castle too in his 'Alnwick Castle garden'.

The term 'physic' garden was supplied by a team from the television programme *Gardeners' World*, which made a thirty-minute film here in 1986. 'This is the herb garden,' I explained. But no, they had just completed a film in the then seemingly inaccessible Chelsea Physic Garden, which we had never managed to visit. We commissioned a label for the garden which was soon installed. A regular visitor called, a happy, benevolent clergyman from Hexham. His eyes filled with delight at this new notice and, with hands clasped, he said aloud, 'Ah, the psychic garden . . .'

The Fancy

The last point of your visit will be to the gazebo in the fancy garden. It is built on the north boundary wall at the end of the axis through the flower garden and the yew hedge. We had often thought that the garden should have a summer-house, but would there be one, or perhaps a pair of small buildings at each corner of this final enclosure, and what would the design be?

The beds of an intended 'shrub maze' had been prepared and some shrubs were even planted. But it was soon clear that there was insufficient space to make a credible maze if the spaces between the paths were to be filled with mature shrubs. So the shrubs were removed and the beds utilised to hold plants in transit, destined for elsewhere in the garden or in the nursery. The area also provided a home for remaining box and holly plants not yet placed, and for new arrivals under observation. Should cut flowers ever be required, they could be found here, since the cutting of garden flowers was seldom considered. It became the 'stock' garden.

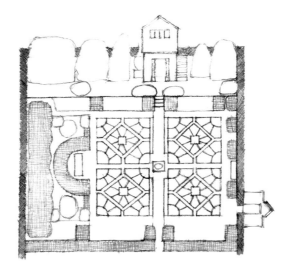

In designing the garden, much emphasis had been laid on the challenge to relate it to the house. This fourth section possessed no architecture to which it might respond and was conspicuously detached from the house by the yew hedge. Then on a quiet July afternoon spent weeding among the stock, pausing for a moment, I stood and glanced towards the house. The sides of the short tunnel through the yew hedge perfectly framed a two-storied window extension we had added in 1988 in a later stage of the house's restoration. Thanks to my chance perfect position, this new feature appeared virtually detached by the yew frame. The image was suggestive of a separate small wing or tower.

This was the eureka moment. Surely we needed to build a free-standing little tower, exactly in line, at the northern end of the garden looking back at the house. It would be a gazebo, and it would be good to build a terrace across the garden for it to stand on. We were in touch with the house again, but we had needed to change its northern elevation before this link could be established.

The prospect was so unexpected and so exciting that the fork was instantly put aside and I ran down the garden into the house for paper. The vision was so clear that I was able to draw the new building.

Some time after the building had been completed in 1998, I related the story to the garden historian and author Patrick Taylor. 'Yes, Frank, but that was how it was always done, and in the eighteenth century it would have been called an "echo".' All over Britain such echoes remain but appear curious since the associated house may have vanished, or been 'Georgianised' or 'Victorianised'. Patrick was a good friend and ally who published several articles about the garden, and included it in his meticulously researched garden guidebooks which appeared in several languages and editions. We had positive discussions and corresponded, and once again he told me things I had not known. But it was encouraging to find that we had discovered the correct architectural solution.

The house extension windows we had used were early Victorian. A chance detour through a suburb three miles north of Newcastle city centre took me past a school built in fine old Gothic style. A demolition man was urgently hitting the building with his metal ball, to reduce it as soon as possible to a new municipal car park. Three sets of stone-mullioned windows were bought for the house.

For the new building, astonishingly, we already had a pair of seventeenth-century mullioned windows lying on sand in the materials yard. These had been purchased from a museum's buyer of architectural fragments, who had originally had a use in mind but in the end had not needed them. Our possible use for them as an addition to the house had not been realised either, but now, at this time of asking, they were exactly what we required.

They would light the small upper room of the gazebo, which was to be reached by an external staircase. The upper storeys of both house and granary were reached by outdoor staircases. Now when you pause at the door on the landing of this third staircase you can look back and see both of the others. The frail old door at the top of the gazebo's stairs was a gift from my sister's old house in Norfolk, given in the hope that we might be able to repair old oak furniture with its broad planks. Michael our joiner was able to repair it sufficiently for reuse and, should it one day require replacement, it will be a very characterful model for its successor.

Below a wide lintel, the ground floor room would be open-fronted, its front edges decorated by a pair of barley-twist columns, the possible location of which I knew. They belonged to Alec, a Cumbrian antique-dealer friend. He had bought them at a sale of the effects of a colleague in Dumfriesshire. They had been recovered from a demolished Victorian house. I had asked, 'What will you do with them, Alec?' 'They might look good in the garden, sunk half-way, don't you think?' I was not convinced and had forgotten them. Now, Alec recalled, they were probably lying in his goat house: he had forgotten them too. He would not want a profit, just the cost, and he could deliver. Marjorie liked the plan, so I collected them the next morning.

For knowledge of gazebos, I was indebted to Ralph Dutton. His book, *The English Garden*, had been a pleasure to read. The clarity of his gazebo theory was instructive and convincing. The building should stand on your boundary; it should have two windows offering completely contrasting views. First, the visitor should see the world outside your boundary; this was termed 'the wilderness'. Then the visitor would look into the garden; this was 'the triumph of art over nature'. Thus, the room provided an opportunity to consider and discuss the entirely different orders presented, which were only separated by the width of the floor beneath your feet.

In the little upper room you can also examine Marjorie's planting plans of the garden, which she designed and executed in 1988, and a selection of photographs of the first two years of its construction, 1976 and 1977, taken by Karen, an American friend who had worked beside us in the art school. Karen was a pioneer who taught photography. She liked to record the human art and practice of doing things, and made many patient visits, fitting effortlessly into the scene like the wind. She knew our cottage garden, and took an interest in the curious English attachment to gardening. Having seen Hartington too, she perhaps wondered how close we might get to realising Dick's prophecy that, following his work clearing the site, 'In six months you will have your new garden'!

The six sheets of Marjorie's plans show the whole ground plan and four detailed plans of the herbaceous plants she used. There is one for the formal garden, one for the physic garden which also includes the shrubs and climbers and explains the materials yard, and two for the flower garden. The final plan is of the trees and shrubs planted in the whole garden. Inevitably, the fancy garden remains an empty space in the first plan. These meticulous drawings listing every plant were a great labour and demonstrate Marjorie's passion for exactness in detail.

In the first gazebos, the room downstairs might have been a banqueting room where, now full of praise, you could sit down to celebrate your host's achievement. Ours offers a different opportunity. In complete contrast to the brightly lit room upstairs, there are no windows here. There is a simple bench against the back wall. If you sit here, you are now the hermit in the cave, and you can contemplate. If you speak, you might even detect an echo.

The terrace may have been a memory of the old sod cast wall which I had so painstakingly removed. This must have held a great amount of soil, for I now had to find forty tons of soil and compost to create a much shorter and lower bank. It had always been enticing to climb on to the old wall to gain a high overview of our work in progress. Karen might have stood there too, for her great panoramic photograph of 1976 closely parallels the present gazebo view.

As soon as architecture intervened, the plan for the rest of that garden fell into place. It would require a broad straight stone-flagged path leading off one step up through the yew hedge to the terrace; the ideal ornament for the garden would be a parterre. Parterres had generally been seen from upper windows enabling a view of the whole design.

It took a few years to prepare the site. Stock had to be removed and rehoused. The site of the path had to be excavated and filled with broken stone and then paved. The terrace had to be made and the building foundations inserted. A parterre had to be designed.

The 'fancy' garden takes its name from 'fancy work', the early everyday term for embroidery, a term still known to embroiderers. Parterre designs were often taken from books of needlework patterns which circulated widely in 'good' households. Nephew Matthew kindly made and sent us a copy of *The Needles Excellency*, printed in 1631.

However, our design was derived from the Tudor rose patterns often executed in terracotta by Italian craftsmen who made plaques which were inserted into brick-built mansions such as Sutton Place. The more immediate source was a small, briefly owned sixteenth-century English coffer. The two carved panels which decorated the front carried the design although they were not identical. It seems that perfect symmetry was not then demanded, as it was later.

A five-petalled rose sits at the centre of a lozenge. The four triangular spandrels each have a Gothic leaf design. A version of the design persisted in country furniture for another two centuries. You may often see three or four panels decorated with a simple diamond motif. If set well away from its frame, it may sprout a few simple suggestions of growth from each extremity. It may enclose a conventional eight-petalled flower, but it will have long ago forgotten that it once nestled among leaves.

The Hartington version respects a modern craving for symmetry and simplicity in pattern-making which characterise 'all-over' patterns seen in textiles. It is a linear translation into straight lines and curves. It is executed in the 'edging' box, according to a Victorian specification. Reginald Blomfield explained in his 1892 book, *The Formal Garden in England*, that 'ribbon' box was usually cut to six inches high and three wide, the plants six inches apart. It was then convenient for the gardener to insert a hardly noticeable new cutting whenever one of the established plants died. Perhaps their small root systems are easily droughted, but they do seem more prone to sudden death than any of the other dozen forms of box in the garden. It is interesting that deaths were common in the Victorian era when their super gardeners lacked neither time nor resources. The specification is not so convenient for the hedge cutter, but when spread over a large square the size seems perfectly correct and satisfactory to the spectator.

At the centre of each 'rose' there is a square from which angled lines reach out to the edges of the lozenge. Our 'Tudor rose' has eight petals. The spandrel design begins from a quarter-circle set in the square corner. Angled lines reach out from this to the diagonal edge, parallel to an edge of the lozenge. Each square centre houses a Warwickshire staddle stone.

The tips of each spandrel are cut off to allow short entry paths which join the paths around the centre lozenge. Arthur paved the paths with narrow stone slabs. Each set of paths has its own slightly different pattern of shorter and longer pieces as they were available.

However, there is no entry to each of the four lozenges from the main central stone path. Marjorie decided to insert a barrier border stripe of different character. Whilst propagating the plants from our stock – an early visitor calculated, with the help of a mathematical mind, that the design had utilised 2,000 plants – she discovered a small quantity of a distinctly 'blue' coloured cultivar. By careful division, she was able to make sufficient little shrubs to create this extra feature. The blue ones are growing to more than twice the height of the little green ones. And they are not planted in a straight line. It is becoming a wavy line which also rises and falls in a wavy manner too. The line may become the long-forgotten Hartington form of the 'Lambton Worm'.

In the late spring of 1999, after the parterre had been planted, a thoughtful regular visitor asked if it would be treated 'à la Française' or 'English style'. 'Please tell me,' I replied. As it was, it was 'French' style, green edges around empty spaces, which we had covered in stone-coloured gritty sand. English style would require a filling of flowers.

In one of the city's art galleries, there is a collection of early Dutch paintings. In one we see a game of bowls being played in the forecourt of a fine house. There is a sunken formal garden in the background. Small beds are decorated with tulips, but only one per bed. They stand erect and proud, each valuable and worthy of study. Perhaps this is 'Dutch' style. It is very dignified and haunting, especially compared to present massed tulip planting suggestive of great crowds or military parade grounds.

We had been very impressed by the knot garden we found at New Place in Stratford-upon-Avon. This was the epitome of English style, a dazzling experience at high summer. The square plot was divided into four parts, much as ours, by narrow stone paths with a convenient diamond-shaped opening at the centre. Each section possibly once had a diamond centre with a diamond surround set upon a rounded square set within an outer square; overlapping shapes became independent shapes. Each line curved and bulged and had an independent life. Any description is guesswork. The plants grew with astonishing vigour and exuberance. Each quarter had a different colour scheme and different flowers and foliage. Small evergreens mixed with succulents and 'summer bedders'. Its textures suggested embroidery. It was flamboyant and suggestive of a summer country dance, Breughel-style. When flagons lie in the grass, dancers will not be in step, musicians will not be in tune . . . It was the antidote to red begonias and 'blue and white'.

However, in the context of this garden, the answer had to be 'French style'. The fancy garden comes at the end of a garden journey which began in a green formal garden, proceeded through a stirring of colour and wafting of smells in the physic garden, then through orchestrated colour when the flower garden was having a party. Now we must return to green as again we meet the landscape.

From the gazebo you must look down on to the parterre. The four parts will join into a repeat pattern with circles forming and triangles joining. You can imagine what colours could be used to build links and contrasts. But just enjoying a green pattern, the vista of the flower garden and its topiaries, and the further landscape beyond, should be enough for this little garden.

The narrower second path across the parterre links a central urn on a square plinth to a pair of benches. The urn was discovered by accident in a city sale of fine art and antiques. It was not present in the saleroom since it was too large and too heavy to be carried up the several stairs from the pavement. It was instead on view in the auctioneers' country saleroom, a dozen miles out of town.

However, two items in the sale were of some interest and so I asked to see the sale catalogue. This opened by chance at the photograph of the urn.

It was mid-September, the season's takings were in the bank ready to carry us through the winter ahead. But in all situations when an object 'speaks to you' you must engage with it. It was a long battle. Dealers came from the Continent, one took a motorbike ride up from London, and finally a museum joined in. It was a difficult winter, but we have been ever thankful that it is here. Whatever items I had been looking for in the catalogue were completely forgotten.

The urn was said to be a lavabo which once belonged to Furness Abbey. Some visitors have said that it may be Roman. Others have seen carved dates which have ranged back in time from early twentieth century to I have forgotten when.

Lewis, our painter and decorator, found the benches for us. He was engaged at a small local village hall and spotted them lingering in long wet grass behind the building. He negotiated a price for us which he kindly paid for us, and then delivered them on his way home from work. The wooden seats had rotted away without trace. We received the cast iron underframes. Michael replaced the seats and took a wire brush to the rusty metal. An inscription was then legible which declared that they had been made in Birmingham in 1808. By chance in an old *Country Life*, I found a letter which showed an engraving of them together with a matching refectory table. They were standard fittings for military barracks. It may be that the valiant men who guarded our shore in case Napoleon should arrive may have sat upon them after duty.

In line with thoughts about time in the flower garden, the bench leaning against the east wall which is very slowly being covered in the miniature ivy, and which faces the sun, could be the 'day' seat, while the opposite one, which is itself being slowly grown over by a yew 'sitouterie', could be the 'night' seat.

The first topiary 'sitouterie' was found in Miss Marigold's old Westmorland garden. My visit was occasioned by a glimpse of the top of her projecting two-storied front door porch displaying the date 1596. We had bought the Victorian mullioned windows, and at that time I was occupied by the design of the extension we planned to add to accommodate them.

The porch was just visible above a high wall which surrounded the garden in front of it. An old iron bell attached to a high locked garden wall door had ceased to raise anybody, and so I found my way to her back door in a yard shared by a farmhouse. I had to ask if I could look at her front door porch. The interview went well and it proved a marvellous visit. The design of that porch in which a mullioned window lit a small room above the door greatly helped my design. She then took me along a box-lined path to see her yellow peony, and then we walked a little further. The land was now falling to the tree-lined bank of the River Eden. The path turned back towards a large box topiary. I went forward to examine it. Its river front was open, there was a seat, but 'Beware!' she called, 'That is where the geese nest.' They had a cosy 'sitouterie' by the river.

The fancy garden is very open and simple; you can absorb it in a glance. You may therefore be more aware of two features which occur in the other gardens too. The first is its sand paths, the second its stone paths.

In the late 1960s, after the National Trust's necessary tree work at Wallington, removal of debris and subsequent soil levelling in the woods, through which visitors to the portico and the walled garden passed, the paths were tidied and consolidated with a yellow limey aggregate sourced in Durham. They were then comfortable and mud-free. Perhaps, we thought, our nearby cottage paths should be improved too, but not yellowed.

We consulted our village 'lorry' man. 'Give me a fortnight. I get around. I'll bring you a few samples.' John was the first of several haulage men who still occasionally call. They have been unfailingly helpful, prompt and reliable. Out of his lorry came six small bags of sand. There was a choice of fine grey-pink, fine but warmer pink, even terracotta, very fine brown-pink, coarser buff-pink, and even nearer to grey. We chose the fine grey-pink. It is very local, good to walk on, and is a pleasant foil to abundant greenery. It seldom needs to be raked; it is levelled by the rain. We use the same form at Herterton.

Marjorie also used the sand to mulch the new flower beds as a defence against weeds. The soil had been so extensively worked and turned that we seemed to have resurrected and given new hope to seeds buried for generations. Weed seeds seem to possess exceptional viability. The new sand cover may, of course, have encouraged the intrepid to walk into the flower bed to see the sundial. Creating a thick barrier proved to be a valuable maintenance strategy. It also opens the soil texture.

Sourcing stone paving became more difficult when demolition declined after 1990. Fine paving had been easily found ten years earlier and we had always bought when opportunity arose. Only the small area of sunny paving in the formal garden, by the front door, had been done 'cottage style' in fragments of stone roof slates.

We had patiently collected sufficient for the main path but now the parterre required more. A good friend in Ravenstonedale nominated a retired farmer who lived, it seemed, on the roof of the world, where Durham met Cumbria and Cumbria met Yorkshire. To the west you look over fifty miles of the Lake District. On narrow empty lanes you can pause and watch a violent storm rise and crash, drenching a hillside. The sun smiles and its golden rays light the rising steam.

This new Frank's drive is marked by fine gate posts and a fringe of sycamores. It rapidly falls to a distinguished old stone-slated farmhouse and sheltering barns. Against the garden wall are neat stacks of stone slates graded in size. We walked back up the drive and turned into a stockyard. Here the neat piles are of paving stones. His passion for stone had recently led him to buy the nearby abandoned old railway station. We walked back through the gate posts, turned left and paused for a moment at a bend. There the trees parted, and we looked into a breathtaking landscape falling away from the road into fields, walls and hollows. Frank pointed out a chain of old stone barns, but the planners would not let him buy one. A little further and a track climbed up to the station. The single line had long gone and Frank had already demolished the little station. There had been a pile of quoins and building stones from it in his stockyard. But the platform remained, passing out of sight around a bend. This was stone fit for any mansion. The huge perfectly cut and dressed slabs were all at least four inches thick.

We needed to go back to the stackyard to look at his collection of stone cottage floors. These two-inch-thick pieces laid on wet Pennine soil would have been no solution to rising damp. Some still retained fragments of the favourite floor paint. Perhaps the colour once made everyone feel warmer. They were good for the parterre. And under a sycamore lay the stationmaster's three-light mullioned window. From his desk he had a panoramic view. This is now available, too, for all who walk into the garden visitors' room at Hartington.

After summer, as the sun drops ever lower and the days shorten, the flower garden is weary and the flower torch-bearer becomes the fancy garden. The ground is higher and sees more sun. There are small box-edged beds either side of the sitouerie which are home to early aquilegias, then masses of white martagon lilies and, for a while in July, examples of the great campanula, *Campanula lactiflora*, almost engulf the growing yew sitouerie with their masses of bells. Marjorie also made little beds either side of the steps which rise on to the terrace. There is also a front-edge fringe of flowers on the terrace itself. Most of the terrace is planted with large shrubs, laurel, box and holly, which eventually may rise in steps towards the crest of the gazebo, which will retain the supreme position.

Flowering is boosted in September by two large plantings of colchicums. A species, possibly *C. byzantinum*, is to the left of the steps and 'Lilac Wonder' is on the right. Behind them are large clumps of montbretia, known now to many as crocosmsia: the old pink *Crocosmia rosea* on the left and the apricot 'George Davison' on the right. And there are two old chrysanthemums, the pom-pom 'Mei-Kyo' and the rubellum hybrid 'Clara Curtis', though these may be affected by early frosts.

Above them on the left side is a tall creamy white cimicifuga (now renamed actaea), probably *C. cordifolia*, then *Aster divaricatus* with small white flowers and black stems, always associated with Miss Jekyll, matched on the right by the high white pokers of *Sanguisorba canadensis* and the rather wild looking white daisies of *Kalimeris incisa* 'Alba', with its somewhat shaggy cut grey-green leaves. At the top of the steps on both sides are huge clumps of pink lavender, with masses of brilliant pink *Nerine bowdenii* flowers beside them.

From spring till winter the terrace walls are enlivened by the lemon-yellow self-seeding Mediterranean 'antirrhinum', *Asarina procumbens*, which positively grins at you. Throughout the season many visitors ask what this charming little stranger might be. Some may guess that it is reminiscent of a 'snapdragon', but its rounded leaves and prostrate spreading growth are not at all characteristic. We found it in Rene Wiggins's legendary little garden, unexpectedly hidden in a quiet suburb of the city. She loved alpines but like many other connoisseur collectors discreetly grew many desirable rarities from other fields too. She was one of the 'Rockers', a venerable member of the Alpine Garden Society, who generally had nothing to do with popular music! She made all her plants so happy that they appeared to be completely climatically adjusted regardless of their place of origin. After one season at Hartington, the asarina was not seen again until seven years later, when Arthur had constructed the dry-stone retaining walls to support the terrace. That summer it awoke in many crevices and has seeded itself happily ever since. It had lived in the stock garden on a horizontal surface during its original summer but clearly managed to leave seed behind. Now we know where it likes to be.

When, in December, the nerines are at last defeated and whitened by frost, you might see us here, well wrapped. I will be wearing one of Aunt Janet's thick stripy scarves, and we will be sitting for a moment in the sun with a mug of cooling coffee. The little bench will have been carried forward to the barley-twist columns so that we are just inside the gazebo. The sun now barely climbs above the ridge of the house. We sit in sunshine but the flower garden below is in the winter shadow. The frost there will not have yielded; that garden is asleep.

We will leave the fancy garden through its final building, a new pedimented gateway which Arthur returned to construct in 2001. He had built the gazebo with his good builder friend Paul and they had built the house extension too. The previous gate had connected the path in front of the gazebo to the high path through the nursery garden. After the gazebo was erected, it was soon clear that the view of the new building, should you approach from the nursery, was not satisfactory. It presented the east side and the staircase. The new gateway connects the path beside the yew hedge to the principal low path through the nursery. The view presented from the new nursery gateway is now much better. It is a prelude to the view of the house you will shortly find through the hedge which presents the gazebo's 'reflection'.

A long broad step leads into the nursery. On either side of this is a pair of rugged stone troughs which came from Marion, Marjorie's mother's cousin. She had been exiled by the pre-war Depression to Staffordshire where her husband found work as a gamekeeper. She lived in a typical three-storied seventeenth-century red-brick farmhouse just a dozen miles from where I was born. It was a house of treasures, for Marion had a keen eye. Every summer she returned to see the North again and sometimes had tea with us. 'When I'm gone,' she said, 'get them troughs away to your garden.' She also gave us some stone setts from the floor of the barn beside her home when it became a house, and Arthur incorporated them into the gazebo's patterned stone floor. And, for sentimental reasons, she gave us a few of the old blue Staffordshire paving bricks which made the garden paths at nearby Moseley Old Hall.

No self-respecting removals expert would consider collecting the troughs for us; it was not an average job. But our old furniture restorer friend, who also dealt in antiquities, had trained as an engineer. Bob always smiled broadly at the world's problems. With his block and tackle equipment he hauled them up planks into his ancient van as if he was playing and landing a giant fish. Mavis, Marion's daughter, displayed all her mother's hospitality, and we enjoyed the long slow drive home along the M6.

On both sides of the troughs is the mint walk. In a narrow border beside the wall are a few favourite forms which attract the butterflies to their mauve or white flowers in early autumn. Keble Martin found 147 British mints. Water mint is here with the grey 'horse' mint, peppermint, green pea mint, the crispy 'Moroccan' mint, lemon mint and an outsider, the giant and beautiful 'cat mint', *Dracocephalum prattii*.

The path leads past square stock beds with rhubarb and sorrel and the long thin nursery beds which join the high path. Here Marjorie propagates directly into the soil all the plants she makes to sell. Ahead is the last group of topiaries, mostly variations upon pyramids in yew and domes in silver holly, which conceal our wooden sheds and a heap of sand. One shed is for stores, the other for wrapping plants in newspaper and for receiving garden visitors. These have shelter to the north from the biggest topiary, a memory in Portuguese laurel of the old round-topped corrugated iron barns, familiar since Arch's Farm. The east side is protected by the holly seedlings Marjorie had prepared for us at Wallington before we left. This hedge is now seven and a half feet high. The principal pyramid is opposite the reception shed at the entrance from the car park. Its height and shape establish contact with the pedimented gate, which in turn relates to the gazebo. A chain of shapes is thus established which ties the garden to what is the first and also the last gate, through which you both enter and leave. This final pyramid sits on a high cubed base and is called the Kiosk. It recalls a childhood memory of visiting the annual fair which came to an enclosed park opposite the church where, in a small kiosk just inside the gate, an unexpected man lurked waiting for your pennies. Unfortunately, some visitors do not read this potent symbolism, and instead of finding me waiting for their cash, they turn away and head for the garden.

After being recalled, they will walk back out of the car park under the willow tree, the 'queen' of the car park. *Salix alba* var. *sericea* presides over the further narrower space which we call the silver-grey courtyard. It is a smaller silvery form of the great white willow, the 'queen' of our lane. By August its shimmering canopy is at its fullest. Some visitors ask if it might be an olive tree . . . Below it is a pair of the grey-blue 'rosemary-leaved' willow, *Salix elaeagnos*.

The north side of the granary opposite the willows is clothed in one of Mrs Rakusen's choice silver ivies. There are silver box shrubs which, since they are not in the garden, are 'rough' cut though they have clear shapes. There is a silver holly and our only cypress, 'Silver Queen'.

Ahead are the high walls Arthur built beside the garden gate. They are clothed with white and cream variegated euonymus. Below them is a border of strong 'crested' male ferns. When they have been cut down, as a winter surprise the bed is full of silver snowdrops. Marjorie has cooled everyone down before they walk under the golden yew arch into the warmth of the flower garden.

Top: the state of the formal garden after the house's internal wall collapsed.
Bottom: the fallen stones redeployed to form the first walls. Across the lane, old
Bill walks into the meadow.

After the topiaries were planted, the narrow centre bed was temporarily filled with old daisies. 'Hen and Chickens' is at the front.

The yellow asphodel lights up in the evening with new flowers which attract the moths.

Opposite: the golden box 'bee-skeps' in evening light. The yew 'needle' is on the left, the yew 'fountain' on the right.
Above: one of the 'speckled hens' is in the centre. Then Marjorie's verge planting of ferns and woodrush makes a 'bridge'
into the meadow.

Above: the two white forms of *Clematis montana* in June. Most of the central part and that to the right of the 'needle' is strongly scented *C. montana* var. *wilsonii*.
Opposite: shapes take on a much more organic character in the snow.

Opposite: the miniature London Pride edging in the physic
garden is *Saxifraga umbrosa* 'Elliot's Variety'.
Above: the three-faced, once painted, Scottish sundial is a
'Bonnie Dundee'.

Opposite top: the first planting of the physic garden.
Opposite bottom: two old terracotta pots filled with sweet-scented thyme stand beside the piers of the central arch.
Above: the pear is clipped twice a year. It is at the centre of an axis of three living arches across the garden. Half of the further square section arch is visible on the right.

Opposite: the stone lavabo at the centre of the fancy garden.
Above: the contribution of pattern-making in the garden is emphasised by the snow.

There are masses of white martagon lilies either side of the sitouterie.

Monochrome pattern with a purple sky.

Four Warwickshire staddle stones surround the lavabo.

Above: the little *Colchicum* 'Lilac Wonder' lives up to its name in September.
Following page: 'toasting' oneself in the twenty-first century.

Part Four

REINVENTING
THE HOUSE

HOUSE RENOVATION

The old house was in a very bad state. When approached for a grant towards the cost of its rescue, the local council refused to accept that it was a house. It was a barn. The air was full of intrigue. The government was going to stop being swindled by unscrupulous speculators who had taken grants to turn barns and garages, chapels and warehouses into second homes, and sold them for profit. Assistance was for people to improve their houses. A house was a house.

The wonderful WI local history study of 1929, *The Troublesome Times*, had won second prize in the WI's national competition to create such a book, in order to promote their new national identity. This gem records the house, and gives the name of the last farmer (a Mr Forster), who moved out in 1709 to take over the Hall beside us, which thereafter served as the farmhouse until about 1959. Well, if it was a house in 1709, it was a barn in 1976, and that was what the council was talking about. If you cared to look up local rates and rents you would see that the records clearly showed that there was no old farmhouse here. Barns were not rated. Councils are not antiquarians or concerned with architectural history; they do not have to look inside, at least not until you have begun work.

With the advice of Ken, with whom I had shared the grammar school's art room and who had taken the train from Birmingham to Newcastle to study architecture, the council's negative decision was overturned. Ken had acquired so many degrees, in architecture, planning and landscape design, that he had become a Ministry of Works Building Inspector. He was a charming man who possessed a clear head and great diplomatic skills. It may have taken a while, but that cheque was so valuable.

There was no front door left to walk through, and no windows. The adjacent byre had an old planked door propped open by someone who forgot to close it. It is the old door which now hangs, back to front, at the top of the granary's steps. (The granary then lacked a door and windows too.) Protected there by an overhanging roof, the door will serve more years yet, though when the snow blows hard, it finds a way in through the odd hole and gap.

The ground floors of both house and byre were a farmer's homemade feast of concrete. They sloped down from the back wall by a foot – in the interest, we supposed, of drainage. In the house there was no ceiling, but the roughly sawn-off ends of floor joists were still secure in the walls, and outside, in the stackyard, was a pile of sawn-off tree trunks roughly adzed, still preserving the curves of nature. These were the original joists, but we had no technical insights into the possibility of reinstating them. The farmer who desired them provided an exceptional load of manure in exchange.

The thickly whitewashed walls were filthy and on the north side they were black and green with thick mossy slime. If you looked up, there was sunlight between the slates. At the back of the north wall a small Georgian building had been attached but no internal communicating door had been provided. It was connected instead by a curious outdoor covered passage to the nearby bothy door. After we had dismantled the little addition, with the aid of a small group of optimistic volunteers from the Northumberland Conservation Group, whom the agent had kindly both recommended and housed in the Wallington courtyard's old youth hostel, I dug over its floor and soon noticed small white pellets in the foundations. After worrying that this might be some sort of mysterious fungus I decided that they were probably fragments of soap. Perhaps this had been a laundry to serve the farm cottages.

Where the two roofs met, the slates were very haphazard. It had been all too easy for the rain to descend the house roof and then divert via the house's internal wall to find its exit, if it cared, via the front door.

You could imagine a tramp taking refuge on a winter's night when the moon was full, the river bright and the sky a magnificent mass of stars. A few years ago, a skeleton was found in the nearby forest, through which we passed when visiting Marjorie's brother, Alan. It sat contentedly on a thick bed of pine needles, leaning against a tree trunk. When you step inside those trees, all is silent; the wind and the snow will not follow you. If you endlessly follow those empty lonely roads, the forest would be a fine hostel. No one seeks you, and only a deer will find you.

The byre section was better, because Marjorie's father, Bill, had installed a new floor with rough larch joists and tanalised floorboards. It was sad that we could no longer ask him when.

No door opened to the north. You had to walk around and climb the external staircase to find your way in. The steps were deeply eroded by the generations who wore homemade clogs, studded with iron nails, which steadily wore down the stone as efficiently as masons' scutch hammers. Below the landing, of three massive stone slabs, was the dog kennel. A fragment of a little door remained in the sturdy iron fittings, perfectly fixed by the blacksmith with lead.

The low door led into the byre's upper room, a long, dark, dirty place. The wall plates, beloved by the spiders, were home to iron remnants, chains, hinges, spikes and mysteries. All might have 'come in' one day, but never did. At three and a half feet high over the floor, these spaces below the slates made ideal shelves. At the house end a narrow doorway, its head shaped by the roof, was cut through the boulder wall. This had led into the house's upper chamber, lit by the two small low windows. Further along the old wall was the site of a generous fireplace. Below, since the floor had been removed, you could see that its companion was barely eight feet from the open front door. That room downstairs had only one window, and that was at the far gable end.

The inner leaf of the upper chamber's gable end was built in the same rugged style as the fireplace wall, though externally it had been rebuilt in the ashlar style of the later low byre and the farm cottages. Shadows cast by projecting stones suggested the possible outline of a different roof shape, sloping much more steeply. Could the original house roof have been of heather thatch, like the surviving example near the Roman Wall, which belongs to the Landmark Trust?

We were sorry when the internal wall collapsed. It was the only surviving piece of original internal structure. But it was good to have seen it, and to ponder on the evidence it provided. Had the probably recent removal of the floor contributed to the disaster? And we were very sorry to have lost the fireplaces. We knew that there was an odd fireplace in the attics of the Hall next door. Unlike the several fine Tudor examples on its lower floors, this one has a single corbel inserted between the jambs and the lintel which projects above the floor. Why the stylistic difference? Did it predate the others, or did it come from somewhere else? Could 'our' last farmer, Mr Forster, have taken one with him when he moved into the Hall? Those generous attics would probably have housed a lot of people, who would have benefited from a fireplace.

In the early 1980s, after old Bill had moved to the village where he died, the Hall remained empty for a year or two. I let out the jackdaws that fell down the chimneys from time to time and flew to a window to let me know. Then the new Trust agent decided that he would take on the Hall and repair it. We got on well; his was an enterprising and lively family. He could, of course, not consider selling us that odd attic fireplace, but if, as he now set out to explore his new region, he should find something suitable, he would let us know. It was a very kind and sympathetic offer, but what chance could there be of finding a spare ancient fireplace in the countryside near here?

Within a week, Oliver had found one. The house it belonged to has now vanished completely, but its image remains as plate 150 in that wonderful book by Christopher Lloyd's wonderful father Nathaniel, *A History of the English House*. When Oliver visited the site, it had already been demolished above the height of five feet. Above the jambs, two corbels protruded, but nothing remained above them. Then Oliver noticed that the lintel had been tossed over a nearby wall and lay undamaged in the grass. We were very happy to pay for its transport, and when the lorry arrived its load included an additional lintel and a spare corbel. There were also two fragments of carved moulding which may have served as a cornice above a lintel. Its chamfered top edge would have provided a base for a fire-hood above, slanting back to the ceiling. The lintel possesses the typical Tudor arch present in the Hall fireplaces, but the corbelling is an earlier feature. Perhaps it belongs to the late fifteenth century, a stage between the Gothic and the Tudor. A Gothic prototype is preserved in Aydon

179

Castle, sixteen miles south of here. This belongs to the end of the thirteenth century. The lower corbels are supported on Gothic columns.

The house from which our new-old fireplace came had been unlived in since before the war, and was much deteriorated. But it was condemned because its gable now stood less than a yard from the edge of a cliff-like river bank where the River Allen raced by below. The edge was almost visibly eroding. We had been very lucky that the demolition men had had no desire for an ancient lintel or two, and we had been so lucky to have found Oliver.

In 1975, we had not been seeking a larger house but a larger garden. But now that byre and house were unified, we undoubtedly had a lot of space. We decided that we should implant a simple, entirely functional structure into the old shell, which would be dry and damp-proof. Life's priority was the great job we faced outdoors. In our earlier exploring and visiting days, we lived in a tent and ate simple meals. If you lay in a thin sleeping bag on hard curved ground, that was compensated for when you opened your tent in the morning to an intimate view of Ludlow Castle. It was the daytime hours that mattered then. The new house was a large tent with bathroom and kitchen and central heating – warm, dry, bright.

The fireplace immediately looked at home in the new simple interior. It was installed against the west gable and commanded the space in front of it. It had been thickly whitewashed, which had concealed the different sources of the stones. The old stone carts are said to have travelled continually to the various quarries locally available, in order to maintain constant supplies to the builders. After determined scrubbing, the whitewash eventually yielded, revealing two or possibly three different origins. Whitewash is very stubborn. It clearly remains in the ruins of Fountains Abbey after 500 years of rain.

We wondered if the fireplace was a Northumbrian type. Some years later, we attended the AGM of the Regional Furniture Society in Exeter. Proceedings always began with an eagerly anticipated talk on the local vernacular architecture of farms and cottages. High on Exmoor we saw that old farmhouses have similar fireplaces. Since Devon is almost in the Atlantic and we are almost in

Scotland, this suggests a wide national distribution, but I have not yet seen pictures of similar ones surviving in the areas in between.

A drawing was prepared for a chimney with a single flue, but first it seemed necessary to personally investigate construction and form. There was one small place not far away which might supply information or inspiration. It was a place we contrived to see once or twice every year and which never failed to excite us, exactly like the journeys we made to see 'Mr Tidy', but these visits were not for gardening reasons: these were for the love of old houses, which once had taken us to Anne Hathaway's.

If we were travelling south via Corbridge, which lay on the Roman road to Scotch Corner, we took a short cut through narrow lanes. This was short in distance, but the journey always took longer; it was an indulgence. Upping and downing, we travelled through a village where Sir Charles's brother, George Macaulay Trevelyan, the great Cambridge historian, had lived. His old house was most distinguished, as was the group of cottages and the old stone terraces. Then the road twisted on further to a hamlet. A large double-pile farmhouse dominated a corner whilst its barns dominated the opposite corner. To the side of these a walk along the field led on to a small church which from the road looked Victorian. Leaving this group, the road climbed to a hilltop, and there on the left, perched on slightly higher banked ground, was an ancient long-abandoned cottage. It sat at right angles to the road, which approached its back wall. We paused here to look up to the only window set high at the left end. It was so special: a small mullioned window whose mullion and side jambs were alike carved in barley-twist manner.

The gable seemed to grow out of the verge and was so covered in ivy that it looked like a hedge. A wall joined on, broke for a gate, then continued to enclose a short garden. The ivy continued and with other things completely blocked the gateway. But we always paused there too, because you could glimpse the house front. Both windows and the door between had drip moulds. The door's lintel appeared to be carved and the windows mullioned. There seemed to be a few old apple trees in the garden and under the field hedge opposite there was a patch of the purple sweet violet, the only place we ever found it. Perhaps it once lived in the garden.

But then one year we came and found that the beautifully carved window had gone, the stone roof too, and the front windows and the fine door frame. It was an inexplicable and thorough assassination. In a year the roof timbers had fallen. The little house looked like a ruined ship with broken masts lying at odd angles just above its walls. But its open aspect revealed that further along the shell there was a chimney flue.

Surely this was the place to look. I climbed into the field, walked around the house and entered the far end of the garden. A door-less back entrance led into the kitchen. The picture rail had almost fallen, and the fireplace was unmistakably Victorian. Everywhere there was a chaotic disorder of masonry, plaster and timber. Having trespassed this far, and full of disappointment, I decided to walk a little further to look into the other room. Through the door-frame I faced a small Edwardian fireplace in a plastered surround. The chimney above had collapsed, the chimney breast too. This room was in worse condition than the kitchen; at least two feet of fallen stones covered the floor and great fallen timbers intervened. But quite unmistakably above the little fireplace, a pair of late fifteenth-century corbels incongruously jutted out from the plaster.

Fired with passion, I saw exactly what to do. I must find the owner of this ruined place, confess my transgression and attempt to buy those corbels before anything else fell down. Whoever had removed all the other architectural gems hadn't stopped to look closely inside. Soon I was knocking with some trepidation at the front door of the nearby large farmhouse which I had passed en route. A pleasant youngish farmer heard my confession without apparent surprise, told me the lady owner's name and explained how to find her, hardly a mile away. Perhaps I hadn't sounded so wicked after all. But, he earnestly warned me, I must make absolutely sure immediately that the lady understood that I had not called to ask if I could buy the house. If she thought that, she would be apoplectic. Times were changing. She had no peace from would-be purchasers, speculative builders and those who were now looking for a little plot of land deep in the country, all on its own, with what unquestionably was a house, not a barn, on site.

The front door opened a few inches, safely guarded by a stout chain. Unfriendly eyes looked out. It was a difficult moment. Perhaps the farmer found some amusement as he directed the 'purchasers' to this controversial door and imagined their reception. But his advice was valuable. And where did I come from? A very small place, sixteen miles away which she might not have heard of. It didn't sound good. But this lady played bridge at Hartington with our near neighbour from the fine Georgian house almost hidden by trees and the copse. She would have passed our garden and heard all about us from her host. Our reputation stood the test. The chain was removed and I was invited in.

It wasn't just the unwanted callers, she was harassed by the council too. The little house was a danger, she must demolish it. She was very angry. In fact that very weekend she was going to get a JCB in and she would get it knocked down.

The price I offered was very acceptable, but the extraction must be completed on Saturday morning. She would call to inspect, and would collect the money at ten o'clock. We were standing in her new conservatory at the back of her house, attached to the kitchen wall. Inserted into the old wall between kitchen and conservatory was the beautiful old barley-twist carved window we had loved and missed so much. She confessed too. Her son had wanted the stone slates, and the window and door dressings, which had gone with him into Hexhamshire.

On Saturday morning, Alan's old pick-up was parked as neatly as possible at the field gateway. Arthur was present too. Under the plaster we found a brick wall which fell apart. Below each corbel was a second corbel, and below them a pair of jambs. These were stopped with quite elaborate carving.

Cash was duly paid. We now had to excavate all of the pieces. But what had happened to the lintel? We poked into the heap of fallen stones, and began to find parts of it. Four large chunks were recovered, but as with the sawn-off floor joists, we possessed no knowledge of how such pieces could possibly be reassembled. And we had to be away before the JCB arrived, since we had blocked the way into the field. And I could not presume on these good men's time on a Saturday for one moment longer than we had agreed. Also, of course, as if by magic we had a spare ancient lintel lying in the materials yard. It was time to go.

That old fireplace had to be rescued. Its style exactly resembled the one Oliver had found. Their locations were only fifteen miles apart. They could well have been shaped and carved by the same team of masons. A beautifully carved moulding pursues the lower edge of the lintel around the inner edge of the corbels and concludes with a decorative chamfer in the lower half of the jamb, twelve inches above the floor. The chamfer clearly presented an opportunity for a final flourish if that were desired. The first fireplace is plainer than the second. As the chamfer follows the rising and falling curves of the corbels, it looks like drapery. It must only be a coincidence that the earliest wainscot-panelled rooms were decorated with various 'linenfold' designs.

Was this modest old ruin once the priest's house? If that nearby little church is Victorian, it may have replaced a derelict ancient one. The end room we had just been working in was the full width of the gable but only seven and a little more feet deep. This is surely where the medieval man sat in a narrow low-backed settle to toast his toes in front of a roaring fire in a corbelled fireplace. He was the symbol of December in woodcuts illustrating the months and the seasons. He was the most enviable one. The front door of Herterton could have opened into a room of similar proportions. Did the thick whitewash conceal evidence of a now-vanished fire window such as existed in this other ruined little place?

The JCB never arrived. That house has been a monument to the quality of the mortar which has kept out wind and ivy, and to the valiant lady who owned it and rejected all of the unwelcome callers, and all of the council's advice. Like it, she preserved her independence.

It took much thought to convey such great pieces of stone from the yard, through the barn and on to the very furthest wall in the house, the west gable. The first lintel was massively heavy, and after the jambs and the corbels had been built into the gable, it had to be raised and then dropped perfectly on to the ends of the two outstretched upper corbels. When everything was ready, and the earlier stages dry and firm, that operation commenced. The lintel was slowly raised on to piles of concrete blocks, one end at a time. Two men lifted, one steadied the lower end, and one placed the next block on to the appropriate pile. Everyone had to lift higher as the piles rose. The higher the piles rose, the more they became inclined to lean outwards when the weight of the lintel pushed against them. As the climax approached, we were disturbed. Pleasantly smiling, in walked the building inspector. Had I forgotten to post the appropriate coupon, warning him that we had reached this stage? Arthur was always a master of public relations. This was just the extra man we needed at this most vital moment. He valiantly stepped forward to help to steady everything at the final lift. Perish any thought now that the measurement between the corbels could be half an inch out. And then we were all jubilant; all was done perfectly. The inspector was the first to say how fine it looked.

The second fireplace had a more difficult journey into the house; it had to be installed upstairs, directly above the first one. The second lintel was not quite so long and may have weighed less, but did the men notice? Its journey took it half-way through the house and then through the side garden door and up the outdoor staircase. It took very concentrated efforts to manage the right-angled bend and then the steep climb up from the landing, through the narrow low external door and round the next right-angled bend into the upper room, which we call the studio.

Then it was necessary to construct a fire-hood to house the two flues, tapering up to the ceiling above which it connected to the chimney. This followed the simple Georgian model of the farm cottages. The Hall chimneys are similar but appropriately taller, with grander coping stones. After the two fireplaces had been reinstated, the house felt much more comfortable, rooms had meaning, a sense of dignity had been restored.

Meanwhile, other problems had to be addressed: windows had been uncomfortable. The original windows had square openings rather than the angled reveals which are nowadays normal. Walls downstairs were also now lined, which made the openings deeper. Conventional curtains did not seem appropriate. Our Wallington cottage had retained its original Victorian shutters, which provided some insulation and security. We decided to have shutters made for all of our new windows.

Reg had been Ernie's apprentice at Wallington. And later, when Ernie had established his own business, he had joined his staff. Later still, he had come back to Wallington, a fully professional joiner. His mother had been the last Trevelyan cook and we had known Reg since he was six. His time was then spent in a seemingly urgent and endless race on his bicycle through the woods. You could hear the 'engine' coming – was it a motor car or a motorbike? – before his cheerful little red face appeared. 'Hello, Reggie . . .' – but he was gone. Reg was resilient and thoroughly enjoyed whatever he was doing.

He happily set about making fourteen pairs of shutters in his own time. We found good brass fittings for them. The wood was Victorian pine, supplied by a most agreeable old man with a passion for wood who had bought a former village bakery to store it all in. Timber shared this copious space with pigeons, since the corrugated iron roof had long ago reached retirement age.

We must have discovered John P. through the demolition men who lived in the same coastal area, where they built themselves large houses. One of them, who was making a garden for his big new house, had found us and sometimes called on a Saturday afternoon. His great American car would thoroughly block the drive. The car park of course was usually filled with the summer's growing piles of walling stone. Unfortunately, it seemed that the demolition men's prosperity was quickly gained and equally quickly lost. People disappeared, and their big houses had to be sold.

John was a stable person, partner in a serious family business. His extra interest took him and his lorry to the demolition of many of the chapels which had sprung up in the mining villages, and from the old pit winding-houses he obtained huge blocks of pitch pine and oak. Pew seats made excellent shelves and from their slatted backs Reg created shutters. Whenever the lorry brought a load of wood, it was refilled with a load of plants. We still had a great quantity of old Matheson's stock in pots, and John had many local friends who must have been emerging gardeners.

When the shutters were finished, at last we could shut out the night sky. Reg's superbly accomplished work, in which every inner edge was finished with traditional Gothic chamfer, transformed the windows as his shelves improved the walls.

Then a further alteration was made inside the back door. A narrow passage had been made through the barn's gable into the house, fitted with a narrow door, which soon felt very inconvenient. Arthur and Paul transformed this into a long, broad corridor and added a new window at the gable end, which had been dark as well as narrow. Along the garden side, Reg constructed a long boot cupboard below two rows of home-turned coat hooks.

The back door had come with us from Wallington. When our cottage there was made by amalgamating two smaller ones, one front and one back door became surplus. Such items were not then valued and so the builder decided that he would like one, and we had kept the other. Reg pointed out the distinctive edge moulding which characterised all the excellent quality Wallington plank doors. He used a further surplus room door to make a side cupboard off the passage. Reg found us the garden door at the end of the passage, which had also been a discarded front door. Where the passage passed through the barn gable, a small portion of old wall remained below the ceiling, on to which Marjorie hung five very differently sized and shaped horseshoes. They represent the luck of Herterton, and you pass under them into the house. They may have been a significant part of the 'treasure' we had unearthed. It was the site's litter of forgotten iron that kept 'scrap' men coming to see us.

After eight years the garden had begun to look better from the house. Each view was less harassing. The plants were making their contributions. Life was extremely busy but we began once again to enjoy simply looking. And then we found that we were looking back, beyond the garden, at the house. We had worked on the house, and in the house. Now we stood back to consider its appearance.

Long before we had considered moving to Hartington we had found the simple but distinctive front elevation most attractive. Some alteration was necessary, but we had been most concerned to preserve and protect its character. Since we only needed one front door, the original house door became a window and one new window was added, but if you did not know which, identification might be a puzzle. The sloping concrete floor had obliged us to heighten the ground floor, which made it necessary in turn to heighten the front door. To disguise this, stone was cut from the jambs of the abandoned doorway.

However, the northern elevation, viewed from the yew hedge, was not satisfactory. Robert, our architect, was ever-patient and resourceful, possessing a huge knowledge of how to make a house comfortable. But, however sensitive and patient he was, his position was difficult. He stood between building regulations, continually evolving, and the client's budget, which in our case was never strong. If we would not accept alterations to the front, we had to accept change at the back. Our problem was the exactly calculated relationship of window sizes to room sizes. It may have been possible to have more light than was deemed necessary, but not less. The modern house, which everyone was presumed to be 'in need of', was thus distanced from the old house from which everyone 'needed' to escape. The size of the large windows we had to accept was emphasised by white paint. We stared in particular horror at a high wide dormer window with an inevitable flat roof, which resembled a great glass box perched on top of the house.

The solution to this offensive problem was the construction of a new window bay with a pitched roof, which was built out into the garden. We spread the glazing a little around the side, and added a small west gable window. The studio room itself, which was served by the new extension, was also shortened when Reg constructed a large storage cupboard at its east end. This incorporated a 'paint pantry' to house our collection of paint tins and brushes and perhaps an old sundial gnomon. He had previously made a similar pantry for the kitchen, exactly in the manner of Wallington cottage pantries.

Then, internally, one great problem still remained: the staircase. We had accepted a simple open stair which rested against the new wall which had replaced the internal fallen stone one. This rose to a landing passage directly opposite the door which served the external staircase. The two stairs rose towards each other. We discovered that this arrangement was very draughty, inconvenient, even dangerous. To slide at gathering speed from the top to the bottom would have been exhilarating, if it had been intended. The resulting bruises certainly amused the doctor.

Alternative plans were conceived which might have incorporated the early mullioned windows, later used in the gazebo, in a further extension, but no design appeared which was satisfactory. Eventually, the possibility was envisaged of using that almost four-foot-wide space which remained between the house's northern wall and the barn's south gable. At that time, it housed the fuel store, accessed by the fine old doorway on the barn's east side. If a stair cut through the left side of the barn gable beside the heating boiler into the fuel store, it could rise to reach a landing, and then turn back behind the boiler and join a short extension from the present landing passage. It could be lit with new landing windows. We would have to join the two roofs to create the necessary head space.

Satisfied by this idea, we needed a staircase. A retired builder, old Dick's brother, recommended a Cumbrian sawmill which delighted in using local materials. The mill also offered joinery services which could provide and fit a bespoke oak staircase. It was a beguiling prospect, but was it ideal?

Our local polling station was a portable shed which always appeared just outside the nearby forestry village, in a space behind the old forester's house and its range of largely unused barns. This had been home to the Massons before Bob retired and they took their final cottage in the Wallington courtyard. The house would previously have been a handsome farmhouse before the forest was planted. We always parked in full view of the back of a large empty barn. Like our granary, its upper floor was accessed by an outdoor stone staircase which looked much longer than either of ours. The image lingered, and thoughts gradually formed of an internal stone staircase matching the external one. Perhaps we could find one.

We had already bought from a farmer in Yorkshire a fine round trough, now in the flower garden. It had been marked 'For Sale' on a road side. I asked for help. Not far away, close to the thundering A1, I was directed to a very professional yard of stone relics. Here I was offered a very fine Georgian stone staircase with beautifully moulded stairs. It looked tempting but this is not a fine Georgian house; what was offered was too refined. We needed something much more brutal and farm-like.

Further calls were made to known and unknown dealers, which took us to a man in Huddersfield. We noticed that in all the towns and cities we passed through, the supermarkets were built in real stone. We had entered the land of plenty. While chapels may have faced demolition here too, we learned that it was the great old mills that provided much of the materials. A mill might have six storeys all furnished with the finest of stone floors. Would we not like some of their huge six or four foot square slabs for our landing? We found the stone we needed and the price included delivery. The pieces were a little worn, with a few damages, but were not eroded by farmers' clogs. They seemed to exactly match the character of those outside.

Installation was a big job. The new landing gave us direct access to the barn's roof space above the utility room. A new major bedroom was created. Previously we had only joined the two buildings at ground floor level.

By now Reg had left the village, and had ceased to do his local extra work. Ernie had retired but we had kept in touch with his plumber, who cheerfully and reliably attended to our mishaps and problems. Peter the plumber had known Reg well, and respected his excellent work. And he now recommended Michael, a highly accomplished joiner and cabinet maker. From Robert's designs, Michael created a massive central roof truss for the new room. He promised that in the event of an earthquake, he would confidently come to shelter underneath it. We might be wise to join him.

He made the new windows and shutters for the bedroom and, for the two windows he had made for the new landings, adapted a set of shutters removed from a local farmhouse by a farmer who shared his wife's preference for curtains. He replaced three of the external doors and added a window to the old Wallington garden door to further lighten the passage. The other external doors have windows too, and so shutters had to be devised for all of these. In memory of the neat old shutter boxes at Wallington, into which the shutters folded when open, simple shutter frames were fixed to walls as closely as possible to the windows, and a matching simple frame fixed around the window. The shutters are then lifted from one to the other as required and held in place by simple wooden snecks. The homemade farm roof lights were small sheets of thick reinforced glass attached to the laths, replacing slates. These small panes lit any dark attic space most effectively and still remain in the garage and the visitors' room. Unimpeded by any window reveals, their effectiveness might have impressed Le Corbusier. In the house these were replaced by modern roof lights, and these too needed shutters. Nathaniel Lloyd did not record such inventions, but it was his book, always a source of inspiration, which provided the idea to resolve this new problem.

I had first discovered an original copy of this book in a most unlikely little library in an adult education college in Durham, and still recall my delight in a photograph of a sliding shutter in Great Dixter itself. This simply slid in its retaining box across the window, pulled along by a hand-whittled knob. It was a functional wonder. From remaining pieces of John P's moulded timber, Michael constructed shutter frames of perfect depth and width to accommodate either one or two shutters, as required, which slide along, pulled by brass knobs. Handmade plaster ceilings are not as flat as they appear and much invisible work was required to make their paths smooth. In spite of the sloping ceilings, they will not fall out.

Before work had begun on the new staircase, a third fireplace was acquired to warm the new bedroom. Our good friend Stephen P reported its availability. A year or two earlier, Stephen had sent us rushing off to see an ancient house he had found which possessed two internal stone staircases. This new fireplace he told us about had to be examined. He had considered purchase, but Stephen has a modern house which suits his life, and so 'went modern' instead. The fireplace was in the possession of the dealer who supplied him with a heating stove, and had been engaged to remove it from a partially demolished farmhouse in Hexhamshire. Much to the discomfort of the new owners, it was stranded high up in a wall which, following partial demolition, had become the house gable end.

Hugh, the National Trust's Historic Buildings consultant, who had considered all our plans for over thirty years, thought that this fireplace might date to the last years of the seventeenth century, coinciding with the age of the barn. Its edge mouldings are very much simpler that the earlier fireplaces but they still have neat stopped chamfers, six inches above the floor, four inches above the hearth stone. Hugh suggested that shortly after that date, chamfers simply continued to the ground.

A pair of late seventeenth-century three-panelled doors with fielded panels was located in Kendal, and a third very similar but five-panelled door came from a house in Ravenstonedale. This is fitted in the small bathroom, just beyond the new bedroom. A small wardrobe room and the bathroom are supported by a huge timber beam in the visitors' room below. An inquiry of the young man who ran the local sawmill was soon answered by the reassuring news that there was one such timber in Scotland, which he would obtain if we wished. It was promptly ordered just in case it was the only one in Scotland. It is supported in the wall beside the station-master's window by the spare corbel which arrived with the spare lintel and the first fireplace. All the ancient relics now have a second home. The room's final architectural fittings were a pair of wall cupboards with two panelled doors, removed from an early eighteenth-century hotel in Appleby.

House renovation has led to completely unexpected adventures, discoveries and searches, exactly comparable to garden construction. When commitment to purpose is established, the search is relentless and rewarding. And, as an ancient relative would again remind me, necessity is the mother of invention.

The stone staircase was the only route upstairs. Note the telephone pole, the oddly angled wall, a little of the farm track, and the car which had transported all of the trophies from the great Matheson's sale.

The ancient fireplace which Oliver found for us, installed in the library-sitting room.

Looking across the landing into the new barn bedroom.

Upper part of the stone staircase inserted between the barn (left) and the north wall of the house (right).

DISCOVERING
1680

In retrospect, it has always seemed lucky that when we married, we had neither money nor possessions. The cupboard was as bare as both the house and the garden we later found at Hartington. After six weeks of urgent work in a sausage factory, I had accumulated a capital of twenty-five pounds but Marjorie, who had managed to find us a one-bedroom flat in an attractive and spacious Edwardian house in one of the best city suburbs, had been obliged to find the one hundred pounds of unofficial key money demanded by the outgoing solicitors who had been renting it. It had to be borrowed from her father, Bill, and later repaid.

Marjorie had work to return to when the art college reopened to students in October and so the loan did not feel oppressive. Having twenty-five pounds in hand to furnish your home felt curiously comforting. However, I was returning to Newcastle to pursue a further year-long course at the university. After the capital was spent, my immediate prospects were nil. An accountant might have summed up the situation gloomily.

Every year Bill treated himself to a day in Newcastle which he thoroughly enjoyed. Armed only with a packet of plain digestive biscuits, he caught the 8 o'clock bus into the city. There was a plethora of tool shops in now-demolished arcades to be examined. Tools and occasional books on building techniques were his passion. And he also looked into the salerooms. He seldom bought furniture, but he saw that as his responsibility, should anything be required. We had no interest in tools or technical books but salesrooms sounded beguiling. I had sat in a saleroom with curiosity to draw the situation and still have a sketch of eager faces surrounding a table covered with second-hand television sets. I paid no attention to the business as it was being conducted, apart from noting the occasional movement of hands and arms.

Mother Evie gave us a bed and her sister Janet found us, among many other gifts, a carpet square, which is still present in one of my watercolours which we hang in the dining room. Other kind people gave cutlery, crockery, saucepans and blankets. My heirloom piano had arrived and the immediately welcome piano stool. Until after the local salesroom's viewing day on Tuesday, there was nothing else to sit on. Eight assorted Victorian and Edwardian chairs were then purchased for one pound. Inlaid or painted wardrobes cost over two pounds and could be returned the following week if they didn't fit. We did not then seem to possess a tape-measure. The second-hand fridge still serves us well.

Second-hand furniture was much more attractive than the banks of chairs and sofas assembled in furniture stores. Designers seemed intent on redefining human posture. Seats became ever lower and deeper. We were moving out of the Victorian era and going back towards that of the Romans. Our heads were being lowered so that our eyes were getting down to the level of the television sets that were then invading homes and lives. The synthetic materials, fabrics and colours were the means, allegedly endorsed by popular demand, to wrench everyone out of the past and into our new world. Our culture was being redefined. As students we lived in flats and bedsits with other people's possessions. The function of chairs, tables and beds was simple and clearly understood. Choice was not our responsibility. But now we had choice. The old furniture of the saleroom evidenced human possession and contact with the past. We might be modern people, but we had not fallen out of love with the past.

After necessary business was completed in the city, we were soon ready to leave. The culture of Wallington pulled too strongly for us to stay longer, though we did not foresee a life in gardening. The cottage was so comfortable after those cold high Edwardian bedrooms we had lived in. It had been our misfortune to experience the winter of 1962–3 when temperatures had stayed below freezing for at least six weeks: even buses had icy windows. The tiny old gas fires could roast nobody's toes. At Wallington, we pioneered in installing central heating, which then was as controversial as growing a lawn. And worse, perhaps, we introduced colour. We had quite a passion for Matisse. While John Fowler, the legendary interior designer, seemed to introduce a sense of Whistler to the great house in the courtyard, Marjorie had discovered the joys of Habitat stores. If the world only needed sixteen colours, their new paints would have offered a powerful selection of contenders. Eight shades of one colour could enhance an exquisitely carved Georgian door, but could we squeeze eight different colours into a small cottage living room? And we were very pleased when the postman delivered the refectory table you could assemble with a screwdriver. It was a new simple form of an eighteenth-century tavern table, and we had no qualms about a polyurethane finish.

The grand Wallington House furniture did not speak to us in the way that some of the cottage furnishings did. Betty's Windsors by the kitchen fire, always draped with Otterburn rugs, exhibited so many unpredictable curves that they were interesting to draw. Mrs Masson's eighteenth-century miscellaneous Scottish chairs, carefully placed below the *Village Wedding*, had dignity, refined shape and impressive size.

However, we were very intrigued by the Persian carpets in the great house. These were wonderful pieces of two-dimensional design. Colours were so considered too; the apple-green border beside the turquoise field was enlivened by reds and yellows, but these details were held in perfect balance with the principal colours, their tones and hues all calculated. The wool glistened and was lovely too. They were so different to the machine-made pieces we all knew too well. Those textures were dull, colours drab, designs boring. Handmade pieces had vitality. William Morris's work is in the great house too. It is a great pleasure to have the scraps of paper and textile Marjorie was given. His valiant assault upon national taste could not have succeeded but his work, still expressed in his Kelmscott house, remains hugely inspiring.

Some of Morris's own collection of historically significant Oriental carpets now forms part of the V&A's collection. In his own designs for carpets he sought to contribute an English dimension to the great Oriental repertoire. In the eighteenth century, architects such as Robert Adam had designed carpets for English rooms which had departed completely from Oriental sources and instead took inspiration from the rooms they fitted into, often reflecting the design of the ceiling above them. At that time all carpet designers also kept an eye on French carpet design, which prescribed the taste of much of Europe. For the structure of his own designs, William Morris turned back to the classical Persian era of the sixteenth and seventeenth centuries. However, his leaves and flowers were informed by the objective study and analysis of natural forms in the tradition of the Western European Renaissance. So flowers forgotten since the days of 'Turkey work' returned to the floor, and idealised versions of both wild and garden flowers and fruits known in English lanes and gardens, such as campions, cornflowers and strawberries (associated as ever with thieving blackbirds!), appeared in many of his compositions.

The travelling library van now brought us books on carpets, often released by reference libraries. When visiting houses and gardens we observed furnishings. In London we discovered that while Kew possessed the plants, the magnificent V&A possessed the rugs and, of course, the pottery and other things. Whatever may have taken us to the great city, an hour in the V&A was the prize.

Houses we visited had sometimes become museums. Furnishings were often assembled by committees or consultants as further evidence of the period. Houses and artefacts interact, but should museum ethics apply to living people? They did not impinge on cottagers and did not concern us much either at that time. We bought Victorian and Edwardian items because they were plentiful and we admired their quality. And gradually we acquired a few items of eighteenth-century oak too. The settle was comfortable beside the fire. Eventually the saleroom produced an Oriental carpet for us. We wondered if it might have fitted in at Wallington. It was important to feel that everything looked well in the cottage. Wallington set standards.

Our furnishings were inadequate at Hartington. The brightly coloured walls of our cottage were not reinstated. Walls had been pink or striped in broad blue and white, butchers-apron fashion, with a deep cornice of lettuce green; there were alcoves of vermillion, a chimney breast of cerise, panels of stippled grey, a wallpaper with a brown and white pattern reminiscent of potato prints, and the canary yellow which had all helped to make a cheerful home for nearly thirteen years. The Oriental carpets we had acquired had answered all challenges, both aesthetic and functional.

Wallington was now 'somewhere else'; Hartington was a sober place. We had to start again. Walls were not made white, but just a little warmer. White in winter can seem to bring winter indoors. Perhaps we had seen enough whitewash. Rugs and furniture were spread thinly on black or plain wooden floors. But matters to do with alternative furnishing had to wait until the house found its final form and everything had to wait for the garden.

There was nothing Georgian or Victorian here, and it had been the age of this house which had led to the style and design of the garden we were making. Period furniture had to be considered, but much as we had marvelled at the educational displays in the Stratford houses, we would never have wanted to live among those displays. The table in Mary Arden's kitchen was truly glorious and would have been most welcome, but the old settle beside the fire looked absurdly unwelcoming regardless of who may have sat there once in candlelight and firelight. The high vertical back and narrow horizontal seat would have required a glass or two of ale to aid survival, but perhaps it encouraged early nights.

We were now very familiar with the alternative means of supply the antique trade offered to the salerooms. There were simultaneous alternatives, and there was time to consider. In the magnificent quayside premises provided by one of the last three surviving 'black and white' merchant houses, the choice was mesmerising. There we had bought our settle, one or two coffers, Staffordshire figures and rugs. But it was in the city's smallest antique shop, a ground floor room on a corner of terraced houses just out of the city centre, that we found two little books which provided new insights into cottage and farmhouse furnishing. There was a reprint of Gertrude Jekyll's *Old West Surrey* of 1904, and a later version of her *Old English Household Life* of 1925 edited and much extended by Sydney Jones in 1939. Elsie Taub was a very sympathetic and tasteful lady who had very little space but sometimes had what exactly you needed, seen nowhere else.

The library had already found us a copy of Miss Jekyll's *Home and Garden* (1900); this had introduced us to her fascination with local vernacular architecture, which underpinned her collaboration with Lutyens in the design of Munstead Wood. These additional books showed her photographs of the cottages and their interiors which had inspired her. With her habitual clarity, she explained her quest to buy examples of the furniture she found at little local house clearance sales. She saw the imperative need to record a culture which others beside herself, born in the first half of the nineteenth century, could see was, by 1905, vanishing day by day.

Sydney Jones spent more than fifty years travelling the country from the Isle of Wight to Lancashire searching out the subject matter for his drawings and photographs, which he published not only in his edition of Miss Jekyll's *Old English Household Life* but in several other books under his own name. He visited many farmhouses and recorded people living and working inside. Both authors found ancient furniture as well as the then only semi-antique pieces which will now seem venerable too. Just as plants and gardening styles became outdated in the fashionable world then reappeared in the cottage and farmhouse world, so did furniture. Then items might be venerated and polished again. Of course some chairs and stools found their way into the wash-house to become part of the domestic washing apparatus, or sat out in the garden. Rain eroded softer parts, sun cracked harder ones, but they too are polished again now. Auctioneers have invented the new description, 'Barn fresh', to quicken the pulse of those seeking discoveries.

I told Maurice Wiggin of our developing fascination for older furniture summed up as 'old oak'. 'Well, that's where we all started,' he replied, 'but you'll get round to mahogany. We did.' He was delighted with the Davenport he had just found. He lived in wonderful half-timbered cottages, where we sometimes thought oak might have looked even more at home than his mahogany. Much as we admired the spectacle of the furniture at Wallington, we couldn't imagine that we would ever seek mahogany. We associated it with the gentry house and the Georgian era.

In about 1990 we joined the Regional Furniture Society, which Marjorie had somehow discovered. The prospect of learning about vernacular furniture which would relate to a vernacular house seemed as enticing as finding out the meaning of 'cottage plants' if you had a cottage garden.

We duly attended our first AGM in Derbyshire and dined with sixty fellow members gathered from all the regions of the British Isles. The air bristled with keen anticipation for the programme of talks and visits ahead. We were personally welcomed by our president, Dr Bernard ('Bill') Cotton, whose great book, *The English Regional Chair*, is the pioneer study of country chair-making in the eighteenth and nineteenth centuries. We later had the opportunity to see his collection of 400 examples, all beautifully polished and labelled, which is now in the Geffrye Museum in London. Bill Cotton's book would shed light on some illustrations in both versions of Miss Jekyll's study. And we shared a table with Victor Chinnery, whose book, *Oak Furniture: The British Tradition,* stands at the very threshold of gaining an understanding of earlier work, and prompts the questions one might ask when making acquisitions. At other meals we learnt what the other members collected, studied, sought, repaired, dealt in or even taught.

Soon we were rushing away to those two great shrines, Hardwick and Haddon. Hardwick Hall was incredibly filled with furniture and embroideries of noble quality, actually made for the house 500 years ago. Haddon Hall possessed a collection of remarkably early forms of cupboards, tables and chairs, passionately assembled on a great scale, a hundred years ago, and often found locally with a zeal comparable to Miss Jekyll's. We observed the refined and the earthy . . . and the unobtainable!

When we began to buy our cottage furniture, it had seemed inexplicably mysterious that antique dealers could look at a piece of furniture and know when it had been made, tell you the name of that period, and tell you what purpose the piece may have served: all of which is not so obvious as you might think. The adaptation of a simple concept to this purpose or to that purpose, which we have now forgotten and could not imagine, was baffling. How many sorts of tables were made? We ate at a 'table', but now we heard of breakfast tables, tea tables and supper tables; and what were 'sofa' tables? And those names were just the tip of the iceberg. It was like discovering plants and plant names, and through them coming to recognise signs of garden history.

We now knew that we liked oak furniture and that it would be right in the house we lived in. But we could see that the field of choice stretched over six centuries. There is early and late in every century, grades between fine and common, city and provincial, patterned and plain. In provincial production, clearly to be our field, styles of decoration, choice of patterns, even colour and wood texture, evidenced clues of regional origin.

With the Regional Furniture Society, we visited the homes of two very dedicated collectors. Just out of Birmingham we met Clive Sherwood, and just into Wales we met John Parry. The first collection would have looked at home in Haddon, while the other would have suited any good country home. And on account of its quality everything we saw in both collections could have looked truly wonderful anywhere. If we asked whether these collectors related their pieces to their house, or the districts where they lived, the answers would be 'No' in the first case and 'Yes' in the second. In the Welsh house, Michael Legge, a life-long connoisseur, dealer, restorer, interior decorator, led our appreciation of ten of the dressers. Taking a drawer from a magnificent example from Montgomeryshire, with a perfectly shaped apron above its pot-board, he explained that if you saw a drawer side attached to a drawer front like that, it could have come from nowhere else but Montgomeryshire. 'Do you see?'

No Northumbrian tradition of furniture-making has been identified, though in the sixteenth century the rich city merchants decorated their quayside homes with fireplaces created by the 'Newcastle School' of carvers, whose members may have been Flemish.

Northumberland is still sparsely populated and is traditionally a land of great estates with tenant farmers. It was the yeoman farmer who emerged in Westmorland whose independent manner and means led demand for new houses and, inevitably, new country furniture. From the seventeenth century onwards, this produced the vernacular house and furniture of the Lake District.

Our idea gradually formed of acquiring some examples from Westmorland, our nearest source, as the focus of a small domestic collection of generally northern pieces. And the hypothetical date of

1680 would be the ideal one for the furniture we needed. Everywhere it seems builders were then busy, and both town and village furniture workshops in full production. The yeoman might celebrate his wedding by commissioning a 'court' or 'press' cupboard on which his and his wife's initials were carved together with the date, and the same motif might appear above the front door, or on the fireplace lintel.

Such self-assertion expresses an optimistic view of life, celebrates the triumph of worldly success. Theirs was 'trophy' furniture. But just as we had seen the rise and fall of the demolition man, we also saw the rise and fall of farmers. Life has ups and downs, like the landscape. Herterton was never a trophy house, and so while we have collected a few pieces of furniture which do express success, these are mixed with other anonymous pieces of a more humble kind, which served their purposes well and acquired equally rich evocative surfaces. They do not reveal their origins since their first owners never afforded the refinements which give clues. Michael Legge might have seen signs which we cannot recognise. Our mixture allows the 'personalities' due space and avoids conflicts. Marjorie composed the order as she arranged her plants. Everything can be seen and heard in turn.

The house is home to other 'trophies' in which we find delight. Floors have rugs and carpets. Finding ones that fit spaces both physically and aesthetically involved a prolonged search. All are old with mellowed colours. We share the weavers' pleasure in pattern-making and organising and balancing colours. We have learnt to beware of the 'personality' pieces which may have too much to say in mixed company. But in rooms where furniture is sparse, rugs lead the conversation. Where the furniture is positive, the carpet is passive but, like the sea below the ship, it contains life too.

One of the first thick carpet books which the library brought awoke our interest when the author proposed that, for the weaver, the carpet is an 'indoor winter garden' on which everyone will sit happily among the flowers which turn winter into summer.

We often returned to look at the carpets at Wallington. We were drawn to their colour compositions and to their patterns, and came to appreciate that the patina of their age-polished wool had helped to focus our attention. The new suggestion that a Persian carpet could be seen as an indoor garden filled with flowers was immediately exciting.

We have never been tempted to become indoor gardeners, though we have saluted the visual excellence of the conservatory collection at Wallington and understand how beguiling Aunt Janet's collection of so many differently scented pelargoniums might be if transferred from the greenhouse to the parlour. And we had no wish to sit on carpets, for chairs had been our first requirement when life confronted us so suddenly with the necessity of finding our own furnishings. But clearly here was a bridge from indoors to outdoors which we had to cross. A life long, life-enhancing partnership was formed.

The planting of Herterton reflects this union, which was not present in our first garden. I have mentioned the importance of border frames, which might be the three-dimensional blue box ridge steadily growing in the fancy garden or the fleeting lines of blue chionodoxa edging golden borders in the flower garden. The repetition with variation of a shape, to emphasise an axis and so enliven one's journey through a garden, is a shared idea. Varying tones and hues of a single colour is parallel to a carpet's often admired 'abrash', that varying of ground colour produced through using ever-new batches of wool coloured with organic dyes. The allowance of space for the self-seeding plants parallels the arbitrary appearance of tiny extra flowers, birds and animals instinctively introduced by the weaver among the principal forms in response to *horror vacui*, the fear of empty space.

Patrick Taylor commented upon the yew hedge's age-old 'tapestry' appeal, occasioned by the use of naturally produced seedlings, which contribute both subtle variety of colour and textural growth to relieve any monotony in a long green surface: and this parallels the joy of a wall built with ever-varied handmade bricks.

Our domestic walls are home to embroideries, entire or fragments. There are a tapestry of magical trees; an early English fragment with applied needlework 'slips' (tiny embroideries) of lily and narcissus and other flowers, which was probably once a curtain; crewel work with the birds, leaves and flowers inspired by the Dutch and English trade with exotic India; Turkish embroidery of leaf and ever-speading tree design; Iznik tulips and pomegranates; a major Turkish curtain; small Persian shoulder bags; a bold Caucasian Kilim fragment in richly coloured geometric design; a pair of Caucasian transport bags, which may depict the eagles at home in their makers' wild landscape; and a Persian bag-face decorated with a large decorative vase with a pair of beautifully drawn birds on either side of it, while four very innocent, naively drawn lambs look up to the scene above them.

There is a trail of pottery including a few of Marjorie's own creations, English and French country jugs and quite a lot of patterned mugs of all sizes. And we have both always liked Staffordshire ware, particularly animals. Blue and white patterned earthenware includes an enormous teapot which lives in the kitchen window. Several visitors have noticed it, but so far we have gained no information about its origin. Just out of visitors' sight is a very large hexagonal jug, a square bowl and a large loving cup which is something of a collage of pieces. There is some maiolica and some Delft, including a large handsome Bristol bowl which is now very much a collage – but one with several pieces missing! If you can still appreciate beauty of design and form in a fragmentary piece, it is still beautiful. You may never be lucky enough to find a better example.

On the stair landing you come face to face with the stone head of a very plain but smiling lady with beautifully arranged and carved hair beneath a simply shaped cap. She may belong to the sixteenth century. A lichen still clings to the place of an invisible ear below her hair, and there is just a trace of another at the end of her thin but finely shaped if slightly battered nose. Nephew Alan dug her out of his garden not far away. There is a carefully shaped hollow in the crown of her head which may indicate that she was once a corbel from a lost building. Alan's garden is not too far from the site of Blackcock Hall, all trace of which has now vanished beneath the present forest. Perhaps the lady once lived at the Hall . . .

A few drawings and paintings hang in the long passage leading from the back door. After Marjorie's William Morris collage, there is one of Betty's little watercolours of a spreading house plant in a terracotta pot with small orange flowers, probably a begonia. It is full of naive pleasure in making colours and leaf shapes. 'Naive' painters know exactly what they are doing. They are shaping, mixing, brushing, testing, but are not inhibited by the rules of those who know better and live in art schools. Opposite is a small nineteenth-century oil painting on an oddly shaped scrap of canvas, of a sailing ship with bright flags and a striking black and pink hull, with pencil and ruler lines indicating ropes. The sky is calm but the sea-green sea is very choppy. The boat has just passed an extremely steep island with a fringe of grassy-green grass exactly on its edge. A lighthouse is also precariously sited on that edge. A trio is made by my painting of periwinkle. It is much the biggest, and has the chairman's place at the head of the long passage. Betty attended my village painting class and we may have had battles over naive watercolours. In this gallery, we all show peacefully together.

In the kitchen is my linocut of Marjorie sewing, and a drawing of Marjorie at work on the old sewing machine in Betty's kitchen. Winter nights were never wasted. And there is Marjorie's drawing of her mother's pantry, in which the shelves are filled with utensils which found constant use, the eggs and scales waiting for Friday.

Beside the dresser in the dining room are two of Marjorie's hen drawings. When Elsie Taub saw the first, she asked for another. Both were completely forgotten until a few years ago when her almost forgotten daughter Joy, now in Cumbria, appeared at the front door. 'I think you should have these back,' she said. Joy – who is now Joy Hall – is the perfect name for that lady. Her very kind gift has given us joy ever since.

At the end of the corridor, the kitchen is to the left while on the right is the dining room. This is immediately inside the front door and so could be called the entrance room too. A long, very plain oak table is in the centre of the room, which is also roughly in the centre of the house. We dine there and entertain occasional visitors. It never matters what their business might be, serious, family or convivial, it is a very friendly table where everyone is equal. It came from a Lakeland farmhouse. Old Dick from Westmorland later sent us a note about it which quoted from a family history, written in 1668, preserved in the county archives. It mentions 'the old table, now in the passage'. This could be that old table, already out of fashion in 1668. Our ideal date of 1680 for furniture acquisitions for the house in fact now ranges from 1580 to 1780, and later. We have given sanctuary to several items 'on the slippery slope' out of favour, as described by Miss Jekyll. One chair at the table could have served in the washhouse, and one stool in the garden. The table itself came out of the barn.

Dick's note included a headline from the *Westmorland Gazette* following the table's passage through the local salerooms. Ever eager to keep a finger on the pulse of the times, it read: *FARM WORK BENCH MAKES £1000*. We hadn't seen the table or attended the sale. However, two days later, our friend Aidan brought us his copy of the *Antique Trade Gazette* which carried a small photograph of the table in the saleroom advertisement.

Aidan is a farmer with a passion for early oak. He bought his early eighteenth-century dresser to celebrate his twenty-first birthday and so we regard him as a prodigy of a collector. His farmer's fingers can run over an early surface and possibly tell him more than his eyes.

He had called to offer us a lift to view but we were too busy. However, as soon as we saw the picture, we thought the table perfect for this house. The style was so simple, so functional, that it was immediately reminiscent of a Bauhaus piece, yet it was clearly ancient. The long framed table, with square legs in natural uncoloured oak, was supported at each end on trestles. However, it had already been sold.

On Monday morning I spoke to the Cumbrian dealer who had bought it. Aidan had already made a purchase from him, and this helped the conversation. However, even then a dealer was on his way from Manchester to see it, but if we telephoned again at midday, we could discover if it was still available. Our call was made from Dick's phone, not far from the dealer. The table had been sold again. We sought consolation with a visit to Hill Top, near Hawkshead in Cumbria, Beatrix Potter's typical Lakeland house. Some rooms would be familiar to her readers, for she painted them to illustrate scenes from her tales. The dresser is still in the kitchen, and there is a very good yeoman's bed with a decorative chest of drawers for company. But we grieved for the table, and later that evening I spoke to the dealer in Manchester. We agreed a price and, after some restoration and polishing, it arrived.

It is almost twelve feet long, two and three-quarter feet wide and the single plank top is almost two inches thick. However, the top surface was extremely worn and eroded and showed plenty of evidence of its second career as a workbench. Perfect holes had been drilled that, if needed, could accommodate our vice. It had been useful for opening and stirring tins of paint on. In spite of its 'restoration' it benefits from having a wall to lean against. We turned the top over and covered it with an old rustic camel-hair runner. Above the end that rests against the wall, Marjorie hung the seventeenth-century Iznik embroidery. This is now very battered, but still beautiful. The technique of long fine couched stitches is very flimsy, almost seeming temporary. Much of the silk has fallen out. Conservation work has preserved the lines of the long elegant tulips, which sway to the left and the right in a sinuous rhythmic manner around a vertical line of sturdy pomegranates. The tulips are worked in vermillion and the pomegranates in ethereal pale, sky-blue, while both are crossed with zigzag lines of pink.

From one side of the table you look out over the landscape, from the other you see a simple farmhouse dresser of about 1780. Beyond the other end of the table is a wonderfully carved Westmorland yeoman press cupboard, which was commissioned for the union of J and E M in 1673. The panels have very detailed carving depicting Celtic knots, which are thought to have been introduced into the design vocabulary of Britain by the Vikings. This is a successful yeoman's 'trophy'.

It is not a tridarn but a 'three-tiered' cupboard which has five doors, two in the top section, two at the next level, and a single low horizontal door that opens into the lower independent part. This is not such a common arrangement as the familiar pair of large doors found in most cupboards to serve the lower part. Some experts think this alternative design may originate from Cumberland. It appears to be a type unique to the north-west. They were sometimes called bread cupboards, found in the kitchen-cum-living-room opposite the fire and bread oven. When a long-lasting supply had been baked, the oat-bread loaves were packed into the cupboard. For some time after this one arrived, it smelt as if some might still be there. It was so difficult to get your head, your arm, your scrubbing brush and your torch into the lower level served by the low horizontal door, all at the same time while lying on the floor. By chance the secret was revealed. Access to the level above was so easy through the pair of small doors at each end. The second and third tiers were separated by a fixed shelf of boards nailed at each end, running from the back to the front. But the broad planks at each end of the shelf were not fixed, so that if you lifted one, you could reach all the corners and sides below not accessible from the low door. The fixed panel between the upper doors in the top tier had a motif of four hearts which are separated by a diagonal cross, the decoration and form of which could suggest a crossed pair of corn dollies. Robert French, whose father had been Lady Trevelyan's shepherd, had lived in the courtyard at Wallington for many years. He was a straw artist and he made a corn dolly for us. This hangs in the large room beyond, which serves as both the library and a sitting room.

The 'library' table is a more familiar yeoman 'refectory' table of 1660 with six baluster-turned legs, the details of which are all a little different in their proportions. This has a wonderfully polished top. At its head is the large tapestry fragment. This depicts at its centre a group of three great trees, and further foliage intrudes from the sides. There is space to look into a distant landscape with cottages, a church and two aristocratic houses. It came from East Anglia and it is our 'Constable'.

A pair of benches with barley-twist legs is on the near side of the table, with three wainscot chairs on the other. At Marjorie's end is her eighteenth-century 'splat' back, and then a probably northern chair with a panel of marigolds and tulips, while the third is a typical Cheshire chair with an embroiderer's panel depicting a central carnation with a pair of tulips and a pair of roses enclosed in vines on each side. Behind them is another extensively carved Westmorland cupboard. It is of the more conventional two-tier form, commemorates S and J D and is dated 1671.

For sitting near the fireplace there is a suitably leaning high-backed settle. Its wide back has two rows of carved panels. There are five panels in each row. Most are geometric in design but there is a primitive floral design at both centres. And there are three Georgian wing chairs from the second half of the eighteenth century. All have provincial square legs. The 'better' cabriole leg has little space in our 'collection'.

Possession of these chairs led to our own involvement in fancy work. A Regional Furniture Society outing to the exquisite National Trust-owned Westwood Manor near Bradford-on-Avon in Wiltshire was especially beguiling, on account of its outstanding examples of needlework. Crewel work, tent stitch, Florentine stitch transformed rooms and furniture, raising colour and pattern above the level of the rich underlying carpets. Edward Lister, the Manor's last private owner, had spent years transforming the house after its typical nineteenth-century decline into use as a farmhouse. He not only collected needlework but took up the needle himself with great success.

Our chairs were found here and there over thirty years, all as different as possible in shape, and all, because of later coverings, needing dust sheets. Perhaps the first such chair to seize our imagination was seen in Arthur Hayden's 1912 book, *Chats on Cottage and Farmhouse Furniture*. It was lacking stretchers and recovered in the Victorian 'plush' known from my grandfather's armchairs, which were not at all attractive. Hayden called it a 'grandfather' chair and our first chance to acquire such a country chair could not be missed. Templates for its needlework were made in Edinburgh.

A reminder of the need for us to commence needlework ourselves came when I was invited to Great Dixter. 'Christo', Christopher Lloyd's familiar name, had also been a contributor to *The Englishman's Garden* and sometimes called on us in summer when he was staying with a local friend, on the way to Scotland.

Great Dixter is a magical house. Christo was a good host who loved conversation. We sat for a while at a large gate-leg table which was one of his introductions to the furniture collection in the house. His father, Nathaniel, had contributed so much early oak, maiolica and a very good collection of rugs that Christo had thoughts of contributing later things. But he was very proud of his collaboration with his mother, Daisy, in making the needlework covers of two wing chairs. (It is interesting that the photograph of one of them in his father's book shows that their work had not then – in 1929 – begun.) He sat every week in one of them to compose his article for *Country Life*. He was the youngest of six children and may hardly have known Nathaniel. All were marshalled by their mother to contribute to winter needlework, which Christo enjoyed showing me.

A uniquely designed staircase, invented by Lutyens during the construction of the house, led up to my bedroom. I did not get a four-poster to sleep in, but Sydney Jones put a photo of the one in which Christo slept in his 1939 version of the Jekyll book, *Old English Household Life*. He had taken possession of it after Daisy died, and thoughtfully added an electric light fitting to the tester to improve his bedtime reading. I did not ask if I could see it, but it appeared again recently in a wonderfully photographed article in the *World of Interiors* magazine. His father's collection also included an early Italian Renaissance-style bed, and two other Georgian beds appeared in the article.

We have been unable to discover any printed source for the simple all-over patterns which would have been used by needleworkers to cover the chairs for the squire, the vicar and the farmer. Unlike the earlier gentry chairs, found in all the books of important furniture, these only rarely appear, in distressed condition, in auction catalogues. Black and white photographs of some may lurk in old guidebooks to lesser well-known houses. The upholstered seat covers of later side or dining chairs are not uncommon: there are many examples in the Bowes Museum. But these are generally too simple to be extended to the nearly seven square metres which are required for a wing chair.

In the window bay added to the 'library', Marjorie hung a rather primitive 'table carpet', probably of the early eighteenth century. The needlework is coarse and there are many domestic repairs. The once nut-brown ground, probably made from acorns, now shows evidence of many later dyes, almost certainly not made from acorns. The design is interesting. From each of the four sides the eye is led into the centre, a sixteen-sided star made by superimposing a diagonal square on to a vertical one. Two most attractive vases, with striped stems above a triangular foot, are filled with leaves and flowers on which the flower-filled star rests. They appear at each end, while flowers, led by tulips, lead in from leafy sides. As you leave this room you pass a finely carved Lakeland mule chest, ordered by A T in 1701.

Travelling up the stone stairs, which connect to the long wide passage from the back door, you turn right from the landing into the new 'barn' bedroom. It is the most spacious bedroom and home to the first four-poster bed we acquired. It may have been made in 1620. It has beautifully turned tall bed-posts, and very deeply recessed panels in the headboard. These required complicated construction, evident from the back. The tester is not original. The bed was purchased from a dealer who had found it in a local sale. I had seen it too and had sketched and measured it. Later, we had made a nostalgic purely objective trip to see it once more, in his showroom, but our response had been purely subjective, and so it came here.

Its length had never been extended. It required a rather diagonal sleeping posture. I asked the auctioneer if anything further could be learnt about its history. Happily he supplied the previous owner's telephone number; they were good friends. It could only be traced to a Brighton dealer who had owned it in 1925. The recent owner and his wife had slept in it for forty years; the sale was occasioned by her death. They had clearly not found its length a problem. I had to ask how tall he was; he was the taller at five feet two inches.

That room is home to our third fireplace. For comfort, you will also find the fourth wing chair and a rather simple Westmorland oak chair. This is recorded in the Royal Commission on Ancient Monuments book on Westmorland. Its back panel has a simply designed interlace pattern, with a pair of deeply carved hearts at each side. Below a typical snail-decorated crest, supported by simply shaped ears, it is prominently dated 1712. It recently passed its three hundredth birthday.

Our best Westmorland chair is in the next bedroom. This celebrates the marriage of C and J M in 1671. It is a virtuoso piece of the carver's art, employing a great variety of devices. It expresses the slightly conservative, nostalgic taste of a successful man. The decoration is reminiscent of earlier screens found in the great hall of any Jacobean house. The complicated well-carved back panel also has three-dimensional applied ornament, including a pair of arches enclosing recessed panels, at the top of which are two small carved hearts. The date appears below the bold volutes which dominate the crest; the initials are just below among scalloped decoration. Long curved scrolled ears with pendants support the crest. Arms have the Lakeland 'dolphin' form; the front seat rail is elaborately shaped. This mighty elm chair was found in a Cumbrian cottage.

This room is also home to the second four-poster, a northern yeoman's bed of about 1680, which is very much like Christo's and complete with the original tester. Both our four-posters are now of normal length. The earlier bed has a cover made for us by a lady in the Borders, with the very glossy characteristic wool from her flock of Wensleydale sheep. This one has a quilt made by Betty and me. Over several years she made all of the pieces which I gradually assembled into patterns. For three years it lay on the floor of the studio, to allow the pieces to be moved around until the order became satisfactory. The pattern was loosely evolved from the design of our best Feraghan carpet, and became an extending diaper in soft red and orange, shadowed by navy blue, on a black and green ground with a sea-green border. Betty then sewed the pieces into larger pieces which I finally sewed together.

Lining, backing and quilting were beyond us, and the quilt languished in a chest. It was rescued by a nurse, Christine, who visited in connexion with Marjorie's welfare after her first hip operation. Christine's passion was quilting; she would love to do the job for us. After an acquaintance of barely twenty minutes, it disappeared into her motor car. Her quilting group were enthused. We had used remnants of 'real' (that is, 1970) Laura Ashley fabrics, together with many other remnants, including parts of Betty's old dresses from the fifties or earlier. Perhaps the quilt does provide a guide to the dress fabrics of the period. Christine's work was excellent.

Betty may have been attracted to patchwork because it revived memories of the wartime experience of constantly needing to 'make something from nothing', to reinvent, in order both to feed and to clothe people . . . 'Making and mending' was the philosophy.

A fragment of a crewel work valance hangs above the late seventeenth-century Yorkshire wardrobe. This was a magical discovery. Having hired a local delivery lorry and driver to collect three tons of paving waiting in Frank's Cumbrian stockyard, for some forgotten reason we made a brief stop at the shop of our antique dealer and furniture restorer friend, Bob Jordan, in Barnard Castle. We enjoyed long conversations whenever I called . . . 'but I can't stay a moment today' . . . 'Well, have a look at this then when you get home.' The supermarket bag was filled with fragments of embroidery and old linen backing, and a piece of fairly new canvas on which someone had begun to assemble an exotic tree from the pieces. All fell into a kaleidoscopic mass on the studio floor. It was a joy to spread the flowers and leaves, executed in many colours and in many stitches. But surely only a seventeenth-century mind could reassemble such chaos into a proper order. For two more nights the detached pieces were studied, and then it was noticed that on the pieces of rotten brown backing linen were now-familiar white images, which corresponded to individual leaves or flowers. They fitted. Then it was noticed that some of the sharp scissor-cut edges of linen fitted to each other too. It took one more night to assemble a five-foot length of coherent pattern, twelve inches high. As many or more pieces remained but no more backing material, so they were returned to Bob. Our conservation expert, Joanna, in Wiltshire, dyed new matching linen and made a complete restoration. Bob gradually sold the remaining pieces to local collectors. The fragments included colourful birds, which will sing in anyone's house.

Now you walk along the landing passage, past the little bedroom where our winter evenings are spent sewing, generally until 10.30, and meet the simple Scottish cradle which is home to Susan, Marjorie's war-time dolly. She rests on her William Morris cushion protected by Marjorie's grandmother's Otterburn mill plaid. She is content that her bright-eyed little face is vacuum-cleaned every year.

The window in the door to the outside staircase at the end of the landing provides wonderful northern light for a 'Turkey-work' chair. The discovery of English 'Turkey work' in the Victoria & Albert Museum was a revelation which led to a passion to somehow find a piece of our own. Such a chair, a purely English invention, brings together in sparkling colour three of life's passions: furniture, carpets and flowers.

Over time, strewing herbs for floor covering were replaced by matting, possibly with a similar smell, but the advent of handmade floor carpets was much later. However, early Renaissance devotional paintings reveal the European taste for Turkish rugs. English weavers learnt their craft from Turkish masters and soon began to develop independent designs related to contemporary needlework. They did not have the same religious inhibition about the depiction of natural forms as their Turkish mentors. They joined the gardeners to secure 'the triumph of art over nature.' English carpets joyfully indulged in clearly identifiable flowers.

The first Turkey-work chairs appeared in the sixteenth century in great houses, but by 1680 they had become universally popular. Turkey-work chair covers were exported to Europe and America. Our example is very like the celebrated chair which Roger Warner, the renowned twentieth-century antique dealer, gave to Temple Newsam House near Leeds. Such chairs are now rarely seen. A few decades later they fell from favour, as thoroughly as the formal gardens, and Turkey work was replaced by tent-stitch embroidery.

Our example was created for us in his workshop by Bob. It seemed almost miraculous when, thanks to a tip from Clive, our carpet dealer friend, we discovered a pair of chair covers in the hands of a London dealer in historical textiles. We had just acquired a '1680' leather-covered chair from Bob, and when Marjorie brilliantly suggested that we acquire a suitable chair and put the covers on to it, I remembered that Bob had shown me such a chair, in very bad state, at the same time as the leathered one. Its lower part was perfect but its upper register needed reinvention. At the time, as in the case of the barley-twist columns, I had dismissed any thought of ownership. Bob loved such challenges, and he also provided the ancient brass studs that Steve needed to complete the upholstery. Curator Neil, from Temple Newsam, sent a photograph of the upholstery of the Warner chair to help. From another supermarket bag, Steve produced sufficient tassel fragments to make the fringes. They had been saved from remnants left over after work on an ancient sofa.

The naive design may have once been inspired by the Dutch flower paintings which celebrated the perfection of creation by combining the most beautiful flowers together regardless of their actual season. In the same way, we meet daffodil, rose, peony, tulip, borage and crown imperial, all together. We are pitched nose-first into a country posy.

We have been lucky to collect a few other pieces of Turkey work which might cover stools. But one is very puzzling. It was acquired from the ever-curious Victor Chinnery, who in his book, *Oak Furniture: The British Tradition,* had discussed Turkey work at length. He had found it in the defunct Wilton carpet factory. It is incomplete and shows burn damage. The colours are soft and English but it would be difficult to describe the shapes depicted as floral. The Cubist painter Fernand

Leger might have approved. It belongs to the early years of the twentieth century and may be a unique experiment deemed a failure. It might have been connected to the busy Cotswold furniture workshops. It sits comfortably on the seat of our best elm chair.

In the studio, the end room just past the Turkey-work chair, Matheson's office partners' desk is the central trophy. Sitting at that old desk, writing cheques and filling wage packets for the job creation team had connected us again to that nursery, which had contributed such knowledge and pleasure to our lives. The desk was serving the progress of gardening once more . . . It sits on an eighteenth-century Ghiordes carpet, or what is left of it. Diagonal lines of an Ottoman sprig of leaf and flowers diagonally cross a field of that unique Turkish pale blue. If you walk in at just the right moment on a summer afternoon, when the room is full of sunlight diffused by the tiny windows so close to the floor, it can feel like walking into the sky. The sky is filled not with clouds but with floating pink flowers.

In the library, directly below the studio, the carpet is decorated with the henna flower pattern. This is reminiscent of the horse chestnut flower, and it is said to turn the central plains of Persia, where Feraghan carpets are made, yellow and white in summer. The carpet has a broad yellow border. When it was first put down, Marjorie was busy just outside the windows, making her sunshine border in the flower garden. This room, which has been the home of many ideas, is edged with yellow too. With a mille-fleur design, a field packed with flowers, the carpet makes a close parallel to the garden outside. It is an indoor garden.

Vita Sackville-West drove to and through Persia when Harold Nicolson, her husband, undertook a diplomatic appointment there. In the hills they collected tulips and other desirable rarities for their garden. The experience of the flora of both the plains and the hills remained a treasured memory which she recalled in her 1926 book, *Passenger to Teheran*. And she appreciated carpets, examples of which delighted us in all the rooms during our precious visit to Sissinghurst.

Graham Thomas was the only gardener, visited at home, who did not have rugs. His small neat new Surrey home, Briar Cottage, was only two miles from Maurice Wiggin's Tudor cottage, where

I first stayed in 1951, and could not have been more different. It was inevitably a working machine which evidenced the busiest of lives. He wrote important books, designed important gardens, painted watercolours, drew flowers with great understanding and, when possible, escaped to sing madrigals. He had worked for the Shah, and been touched by carpets. He was intrigued by the rare and mysterious seventeenth-century Persian garden carpets such as the hugely important one which belonged to Sir William Burrell, still to be seen in the Burrell Collection in Glasgow. He wondered if they could possibly have had any influence on seventeenth-century European garden designs. He thought I should write a book on the subject, but it would be a mighty subject and we are not academics. He made a good cup of tea, and found us one or two plants, which were simply wrapped in newspaper.

We had called on Mary McMurtrie on our journey to Crathes, hoping to buy some of her pinks. She was a delightful and kind lady who answered her back door and promptly invited us to share her tomato soup in the kitchen. We retreated to Marjorie's prepared picnic but were happy to see her house afterwards. She had painstakingly restored the building and was justifiably pleased with her achievement. The library made a great impression. There she wrote her four pamphlets, *Wild Flowers of the Algarve*, and her books, *Old Cottage Pinks*, *Wild Flowers of Scotland* and *Scots Roses of Hedgerows and Wild Gardens*, and also painted watercolours to illustrate them. We found a name for a haunting little red laced pink we had found in a neighbouring village; it is Cockenzie, named in 1723. The room that held her library had most distinguished Turkish kelims. One room was furnished only with one ancient carpet, and that was incomplete. That dramatic gesture was a homage worthy of such a piece.

We much admired the work of Sir Hardy Amies. He had begun his Cotswold garden barely two years before work began at Hartington, but the photograph of his garden in *The Englishman's Garden* showed very firm and positive design. The summer-house he designed in Cotswold style is a gem. Whilst our garden may have been the youngest in the book, his could have been the smallest. At the launch of *The Englishman's Garden*, Rosemary Verey, who co-edited the book with Avilde Lees-Milne, had commented that I did at least look like a gardener, which may have been some sort of praise. So many of the other contributors had very serious other commitments to contend with. Hardy Amies had bought the small 1840 school, in the same south Cotswold village adopted a few years earlier by his sister, as an escape from his London world. Spinster sister and bachelor brother were almost neighbours.

Cotswold materials and style lived on, and he explained that his house policy had been to 'step down' on the Victorian and to 'step up' the Jacobean. He was entangled in the seventeenth century and talked of its politicians and personalities. Sitting in his handsome long high sitting room, you could not have guessed that it could once have been a school room. Its height at the far end was matched by a tapestry which filled the space above an immaculate seventeenth-century serving table. Mullion windows with pieces of medieval stained glass attached were behind us and a bust of Charles I kept watch. An elaborately carved Jacobean fireplace faced us. The best and prettiest of Ushak carpets was at our feet, while examples of his needlework were everywhere.

We walked into his garden through the tall glass doors of his dining room. The summer-house was of course in perfect alignment with the doors. He apologised that autumn was the garden's worst season. His passion for straight lines, symmetry and order, perfectly clipped box hedges, the scents of roses, a sense of colour, for which John Fowler had been his inspiration, and the garden's perfect condition, all demonstrated that no apology was required.

He was in his eighties and carried a stick, but proposed that we should walk a little way through the village to see the houses and visit his tennis court and, more importantly, his pavilion, a small converted barn which was also his library. Here we sat on wainscot chairs beside a rustic fireplace he had improvised with a heavy old arch-shaped lintel. His barn conversion was as accomplished as that of his house. We discussed furniture and then drank whisky. Knowing little of whisky, I had to guess that this must have been the very best, and the quantity offered was the most generous imaginable. It was extremely good. Then, mindful of his Sunday lunch which his sister was cooking, we set off to retrace our steps.

His stick was no longer adequate and he took my arm. That was a good idea. We were locked together in mutual support, both a little unsteady on our legs. But no traffic stirred in this quiet place. He had pointed out which television star lived there, and who else lived here, but no one was seen. I wondered whether this was how everyone returned after a visit to the tennis court. I also wondered whether, as we passed, anyone noticed and was curious about the great man's newest companion. Lunch smelt delicious and I was offered a chair at the table. Hardy's hospitality was impeccable. He sought perfection in whatever he did. But I thought it better to open the car's windows and take some air as I travelled through exquisite Cotswold villages on to Broadway.

There I visited Snowshill. It is not a farmhouse, but in the context of houses, people and collecting, it represents an extreme position. After all of his collections had been accommodated, there had been just enough space at the very end, perhaps it was next door, for Charles Paget Wade to squeeze in a personal bed. Had there been time for sleeping, though, for that driven man who from childhood had needed to save everything beautiful that needed to be saved? The beds, the country furniture, the Turkomen bags, the carpets I knew were wonderful, but how little I knew about many of his other collections, such as Japanese armour and bicycles. The sunny autumn afternoon and the prettily planted garden outside seemed extraordinary when you re-emerged because, unlike that inconceivable interior, they were not at all extraordinary. What might have happened if Mr Wade had discovered that some plants and garden concepts needed to be saved?

The return home was made through the quieter parts of Shropshire to enjoy the last of the 'black and white' cottages. It is then a long time before the wild green empty landscape of Northumberland is reached. The isolated farms keep a discreet distance from the highway, different to the more comfortable Midlands and the jewel-like Cotswolds.

Such a journey provides time to reflect. The homes of people who cherish ideals and feel obliged to make, to create, to design, will each be different and unpredictable: and equally as expressive as their various great achievements, which we celebrate. Although we have only been gardening and recreating an old house, ours has not been an average life either. The furnishing of this old farmhouse may not be wholly completed, and the exact order of all the parts wholly finished: progress is unhurried and erratically woven around many other demanding preoccupations. Yet all may now be in tune and in time with the place. The furnishings are not of the gentry sort, and the condition of this or that is not always perfect. Many items have seen rustic use, an odd one may have suffered misuse, but if something seems to welcome us, we welcome it in return. The unpredicted assemblage does reflect our life and is full of memories of people, places, journeys, discoveries; apart from the piano, everything has been collected from somewhere.

It does now feel comfortable. The garden seems to be adjusted to the house. The house was always happily a part of the landscape, and if what is inside is fitting for the exterior, and the gardens fit in too, a unity should exist. But whereas the landscape is not at all refined by human taste, our contributions, indoors and outdoors, have been wholly fashioned by aesthetic considerations. To achieve a sense of unity or balance between natural and man-made orders has been our quest. To achieve a unity of purpose and execution is what the artist dreams of. It may elude him, but in the great examination of time, evaluation will be made. He may never know whether he fails or succeeds. For him it is just essential to follow the quest. Others may judge the achievement.

The new passage from the back door with Marjorie's horseshoes above. On the left is a very long embroidered Turkish curtain.

The library table, benches and bookshelves and, the product of our winter occupation, two embroidered chairs.

The hearth settle displays ambitious carving. The corn dolly hangs behind the chair and on the wall to its left, in the window alcove, Marjorie hung a primitive 'table' carpet.

In the studio directly above the library is the second equally ancient fireplace. In the centre is Matheson's office desk, still busy, and on the floor some of the collected seed-heads are drying.

Top: work proceeds for the next chair.
Bottom: the design is worked in Florentine stitch.

Top: Marjorie makes notes at the library table.
Bottom: the notes and plans proliferate.

Top left: a huge maiolica pot in the dining room, once filled with Aqua di Endiv?
Top right: a panel in the settle filled with tulips.
Bottom: an early, possibly Italian, fragment carved with dolphins and fountains, a cherub
and a neptune. The muntins sport hanging bunches of figs.

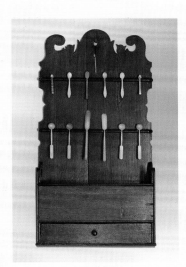

Top left: detail of the silk Ottoman embroidery of tulips and pomegranates.

Top right: Marjorie made this silk cushion in the 1960s.

Bottom left: the Turkey-work chair of 1680.

Bottom centre: homemade bone spoons fill a rack formerly in Jack Young's collection.

Bottom right: the Westmorland three-stage 'court cupboard'.

Above: a large Frank Cubist still life painted in 1959.
Opposite: a later still life from 1962.

Under the arches with the falconer (1994).

LOOKING BACK

What had it meant to leave Wallington? Our first garden had been an excellent workshop in an ideal position. Life was spent in a little 'cul-de-sac', down a path from a great and vibrant place which we could see and hear. We had thrived in a culture where art was at home: it had been liberating and open. But we needed to expand, and to explore further. Perhaps we had begun to feel a little stifled.

Hartington had great appeal. It was very close, it seemed to belong historically, and it certainly looked as if it needed all the energy we possessed. This had been generated in those vital years of seeing and doing we had spent at Wallington. Hartington also appealed because it was so different. It had air, space, and a great deal of silence, perhaps mystery.

Here, apart from the wind, any sense of bustle is created by farmers and their various movements. The open landscape is attractive, but completely lacks a cultivated picturesque quality like that so carefully created around Wallington. That landscape was greatly admired as a work of art in the eighteenth century, and has been admired ever since. The landscape at Hartington has the natural beauty of contours and trees, and a little river, but is possessed by other rituals of busyness. It is unobtrusively and exclusively at work. It has a different culture, not motivated in any way by art.

Farmers are marvellous workers whose craftsmanship and orderliness are most impressive, and they are wonderfully in touch with the rhythms of time. It might have been understandable if some thought that a garden could not be made here. It was not an oasis, it could not flourish. But no doubt the retired farmer who warned that our project could not succeed was concerned because he knew that our 'land' was just stone, as unsuitable as if we were beginning work in the Sahara. He would not think that the project was philosophically in the wrong place, and that gardens belonged to other places, like Wallington.

Another old lifelong farmer, with generations of farmers before him, clearly felt very uncomfortable, and did not progress far inside Arthur's walls. He felt he was imprisoned, for at Hartington the order was air, openness, space. Old Bill had been a lifelong farmer with generations before him too, and all his friends were farmers. He seemed a very honest old man, but was very suspicious. He liked an occasional chat with our team to probe into their tasks. The team was happy and 'on our side', and may sometimes have teased him. 'Oh, this is where we are going to make the new swimming pool, Bill . . .'

And then when more walls had been built, and the forms of the garden had begun to emerge, a charge came from the other direction. A painter friend stated that the garden was 'miles over the top', and advised that it would be better for us to concentrate on artistic pursuits, meaning taking out the paint brushes again. Did the garden look out of place beside the house, or perhaps with the landscape? The advice was kindly meant, for our benefit, and we remained good friends. It was a last trumpet call to rejoin the ranks. We have since received compliments from the same source.

We were aware of the special character of our new environment, and took many steps to ensure that our work 'fitted in' with this simple, peaceful place, almost on the moors, far away from the world of great designers. We incorporated the trees and shrubs of the lanes and the landscape: green remains our fundamental colour.

Graham Thomas was not happy with foliage of other colours in an 'English' green landscape. We came well equipped, by Matheson's, with purples, browns and reds, but Marjorie found that they just did not fit, though the yellows and the greens variegated with white or yellow were of great importance, particularly in the hidden flower garden. In the urban environment, where red brick dominates the landscape, all the other colours can certainly sing.

We were not inhibited. We had simply packed our culture with our furniture and brought it with us, and have been as busy as everyone else for almost four decades. It is difficult to step outside, and to see what is inside our walls as objectively as everyone else can. Visitors often tell us that they have enjoyed looking. They enjoy the silence, and some find a sense of peace. This begins in the physic garden, then continues in the very open formal garden, and continues in the warm flower garden, which they share with the birds and very many insects. We get reports from the bird watchers, and an occasional member of the Bumblebee Preservation Trust. The afternoon sun is warm if you sit on the bench in the fancy garden and look at pattern, or the great lavabo. The British Sundial Society keeps an eye on the physic garden. Perhaps there is a small oasis here now which did not exist before.

Holidays have not been a part of life, but it has always been a refreshing pleasure to take a day away in summer or autumn. When we return in the evening, having been absorbed in quite different things, we catch a glimpse of it all before vision so quickly resumes normality. For that moment we are pleased that Herterton now takes its place beside the other old places we have occasionally seen here and there which we have admired. For us, it is now what we would like to find along a narrow country lane that really goes nowhere urgently. It should look a little different. A house from somewhere in the past should have a garden which evidences a past too. If the people who live there have been busy making and shaping, you have something to ponder.

Here you will still hear English plant names, where Latin accuracies are less essential, though if required, well-intentioned Latin possibilities are available for foreign visitors and English alike. The flowers belong to the countryside and to the cottage, so often the source of this collection. It is not a simple cottage garden: it has a broader concern, and presents evidence of the delights which history has provided for the gardens of such a place. We call it a 'country' garden. The old names still persist and fascinate, and we enjoy being very puzzled by some which visitors from other regions sometimes quote.

A few years ago a very famous garden writer called, whom we had not met before. His opinions had been quoted by friends and callers so often for years and years. He asked if we would mind if he wrote about the garden. I took him to see it all. He had worked for Margery Fish in summer holidays and he knew a lot about old flowers, and a lot about alpines too. Presently, we were resting our elbows on the stone sill below the old mullioned windows in the gazebo, and gazing, as we should, over the garden below, and beyond. We had looked at Karen's photos and Marjorie's plans. He turned and simply asked, 'Are you pleased with this?' It was so gentle, so direct, so simple, so challenging. No one had ever asked that before. It was a real question.

We looked over the parterre, with topiarised box shrubs on the left and the emerging sitouerie on the right; over Arthur's new gateway of 2001, and the projecting water tables above its pediment which I had had to draw so many times in preparation; and at the two outdoor staircases, the willows and then the yew arches, and the buttresses beyond the yew hedge; the great cones of golden holly, and the two yellow-leaved trees, the alder and the nut; and at the securely united roofs of barn and house which frame the flower garden, and hints of flower colour; at the house's new north elevation, over the roof between the new chimneys, to the landscape beyond the river: and I found that I had to look back in return, and say, 'Yes.'

His subsequent article expressed real appreciation, and was of great benefit to us. We were reassured that we might have 'got it right'.

But, he asked, how did we keep everywhere 'so clean, so tidy'? Well, there is a little rule, 'Never pass the grass!' This means that should you be strolling or striding along a little path on a summer morning, thinking of this, or planning that, or even about to rush away, and the sun should illuminate a little tuft of bright new grass just beginning life's journey, exactly at your foot, you should stop. You halt, banish the thoughts, stop the journey, bend down, and carefully and firmly remove it. It belongs to the meadow and, should you ignore it, it will make a meadow of your path or your flower bed almost before you will have time to repeat your journey. The farmers too will not permit grass to grow between the cobbles of their 'front-of-the-byre' paving. It sounds like a rule for children, and can be difficult for sensible adults to follow. Your resolve will be tested again tomorrow.

Simple rules are the best. Marjorie, who was born in the tiniest of cottages, into a very busy family, knows a lot of country secrets, about what should be done, and how things should be kept, from sweeping paths to polishing door knobs and constantly cleaning stone paths and outdoor staircases. She was instinctively able to appreciate culture around her, and her independence and education taught her more. Why, she asked, should small places not be as beautiful as great places? She was determined that everything should be done thoughtfully and properly here.

When it came to furnishing, we discovered that we shared a youthful passion for the same book. *Wind in the Willows* had never been forgotten, and ideas we share about furniture may have crept unseen into our lives even then. Hartington with its wild river, its meadows, its copse, its seldom seen people, may even have something in common with the scenes so beautifully depicted in *Wind in the Willows*. But we very much hope that the characters depicted will never think of moving into our garden here. Mole occasionally passes up and down the heavily composted space between the shrubs and the shelter hollies, on the west side of the flower garden, when everything is soft and juicy, in spring or autumn.

Badger's front door was so fortunately discovered on the terrible night of the blizzard when everybody should have been indoors, and not lost in the wild dark wood. Today, many who live in the countryside will know the terror of the blizzard when you are twenty miles from home, and the men of the road have sensibly given up the battle and retired for the night to take a meal and a rest, before looking at the world again with clear eyes in the morning. And if you are in the copse in moonlight, it is a foreign place. You can no longer distinguish west from north, even though you thought you knew where you were before you turned to look a moment ago. Landmarks are not there, paths are different. You do not identify the patches of moonlight and everything else is just black, neither space nor matter.

Kenneth Grahame clearly knew about farmhouse kitchens, and the joys of farmhouse feasts. E.H. Shepard's lovely drawings showed he knew the scenes that both Jekyll and Jones had illustrated, she in the first, he in the later, revised and expanded edition of *Old English Household Life*. *Wind in the Willows* was first published in 1908, but the Shepard illustrations were only added in 1931. We hope that the drawings of both Shepard and Sydney Jones will not be forgotten. Contemporary illustrations of new editions of *Wind in the Willows* are rather different.

Badger's lantern leads us all down into the kitchen, which is full of warmth and firelight. The unexpected guests receive pyjamas and dressing gowns, and warm themselves at the fire, where a pair of high-backed settles is provided. Supper is served on the long trestle table, on one side of which is the long bench. We then see host and visitors, suffused with food, lying back in old 'comfy' chairs, on the other side of the table. They are silhouetted against a wonderfully equipped long Welsh dresser on which rows of plates gleam in the firelight. Everything which might have been considered appropriate is there. There are glimpses of a study, a bedroom and a storeroom.

As furnishing began at Hartington, we sometimes asked whether this chest of drawers, or that old chair, would have fitted into that secret world of *Wind in the Willows* because, if so, it would surely fit in here. It was a very subjective test for there was no inventory available against which to check. After we joined the Regional Furniture Society, our selection became more scientific.

In the autumn, the studio begins to remind us of one of Badger's storerooms. The pale blue carpet begins to be covered, and the tops of chests, and the settle, and the tops of other things too, with torn sheets of newspaper. It is now the time of Marjorie's seed harvest. The papers have bold pencilled labels reminding us that the seed-heads, all so different, which rest on them, are of pink clary or white clary, yellow agrimony or white agrimony, the yellow peony or the red tulip. Gradually the seeds will be released and, when the room is not too cold to work in, put into packets and labelled, then placed into the seed boxes, which will reappear in the packing shed in time for the first callers in April or May.

Seeds are collected from special plants which it may not be possible to offer in the nursery beds, and there will be seeds of annuals and biennials which always perform best if raised directly from seed. Some may travel as far as Russia, though I am not sure that they should. It is one of Marjorie's 'secondary' occupations in a house at work, where jobs must not be forgotten.

People sometimes ask if there may be a time when everything is done, but we cannot say. Longevity and fitness for purpose is guaranteed to no one. Everything is not done yet. Some gardening commitments go on for a long time.

Miss Shaftoe drove slowly 'up the bank' to do her old friend's vegetable garden in the village until she was ninety-three, and then, one morning, she died. She had retired from her smallholding and taken a tiny cottage in the Wallington courtyard. A tradesman friend recalled her roofing adventure some time before retirement. She climbed up the ladder to attend to the slates, for who else would? But, on this occasion, it was windy. She had hardly climbed on to the roof, when the wind blew her ladder away. She lived beside the narrowest and loneliest of roads, and remained where she was until a neighbour drove by and recognised an unusual note of urgency in those friendly waves from the roof, and she was rescued. It was such a lonely place that if someone did call and looked inside, for the door would be open, her poor cats took fright up her chimney. She had done good things, including saving an ancient church. Now she had been saved to do just a little more gardening. Had she managed to get the potatoes in?

Our last sight of Reginald Kaye was of him hard at work. His friendly son told us that he would be just too busy to see us. He was the great fern expert and at his nursery in Silverdale there was always something never seen before to tempt us, and his alpines and perennials had special qualities too. His son now did much of the propagating, though he did not handle the precious ferns, and he served us perfectly well. Reginald was steadily working from his knees on his new four-acre rock garden. Reginald was then ninety-four.

Our judgement seems to have been right, one acre has been perfectly sufficient, for we have a very intensive style. Two people are quite essential, one would not be enough. While I look after the cutting and trimming and digging, Marjorie takes care of all the flowers, flower beds and nursery stock. All the seasons yield their prizes and present their problems. We anticipate them all with pleasure. The calendar is full. The world indoors follows the world outdoors.

But as winter regains the upper hand and we await the disorders, damages and dislocations it may heap upon us, we can only hope that when the blizzard returns it will avoid our weekly shopping day. We have not yet learned to be as provident as Badger was. And if we should admit any fearfulness of nature's resources, could that possibly indicate that after all our years in the front line of resistance, we too, like the mythical admiral who took on one battle too many and Lady Pauline's ancient beech whose name is forgotten, may also be getting old?

The blizzard is here.

Snow brings topiaries to life at this cold dead time of year.
The spirals in the blue beds assume a new importance.

Above: this is the third 'living arch' in the physic garden. It is -5˚C
in January, but we are coming out (2013).
Following page: plants for customers in the packing shed.

Bibliography

AND INDEX

BIBLIOGRAPHY

Author's Note

I have mentioned most of these books in the text. The few that I haven't mentioned have nevertheless been important to us.

Amherst, Alicia (Lady Rockley), *A History of Gardening in England*, 1895

Austin, Alfred, *The Story of my Garden*

Bell, Quentin, *Elders and Betters*, 1989

Blomfield, Reginald, *The Formal Garden in England*, 1885

Bosanquet, R.E. (editor), *In the Troublesome Times*, 1929 (Cambo Women's Institute Book, 1922)

Bower, H., *Textiles at Temple Newsam: The Roger Warner Collection*, 2000

Chinnery, Victor, *Oak Furniture: The British Tradition*, 1979

Cotton, Bernard D., *The English Regional Chair*, 1990

Diehl, Gaston, *Henri Matisse*, 1958

Dilley, Arthur Urban, *Oriental Rugs and Carpets: A Comprehensive Study*, revised by Maurice S. Dimand, 1959

Ditchfield, P.H., *The Manor Houses of England* (illustrated by Sydney Jones), 1983

Dutton, Ralph, *The English Country House*, 1935

Dutton, Ralph, *The English Garden*, 1937

Earle, C.W. (Mrs), *Pot Pourri from a Surrey Garden*, 1897

Edwards, J., *Crewel Embroidery in England*, 1975

Fish, Margery, *Cottage Garden Flowers*, 1961

Fish, Margery, *Carefree Gardening*, 1966

Glendinning, Victoria, *Vita*, 1983

Gould, Sabine Baring, *Old Country Life*, 1889

Grahame, Kenneth, *The Wind in the Willows*, illustrated by E.H. Shepard, 1931

Hellyer, Arthur, *Amateur Gardening*, 1963

Hentzner, Paul, *Travels in England during the Reign of Queen Elizabeth*, 1894

Heyden, Arthur, *Chats on Cottage and Farmhouse Furniture*, 1912

Hodgson, J., *History of Northumberland*, 1820

Huish, Marcus, *Happy England* (illustrated by Helen Allingham), 1909

Jekyll, Gertrude, *Home and Garden*, 1900

Jekyll, Gertrude, *Old West Surrey*, 1904

Jekyll, Gertrude, *Old English Household Life*, 1925

Jekyll, Gertrude, *Old English Household Life*, 2nd edn., 1931 (extended and illustrated by Sydney Jones)

Keble, Martin, W., *The Concise British Flora in Colour*, 1965

Lloyd, Nathaniel, *Garden Craftsmanship in Yew and Box*, 1925

Lloyd, Nathaniel, *A History of the English House from Primitive Times to the Victorian Period*, 1931

Robinson, William, *The English Flower Garden*, 1883 Rohde, Eleanour Sinclair, *The Old English Herbals*, 1922

Rohde, Eleanour Sinclair, *The Scented Garden*, 1931

Rohde, Eleanour Sinclair, *The Story of the Garden*, 1936

Rohde, Eleanour Sinclair, *Herbs and Herb Gardening*, 1946

Royal Commission on Historical Monuments (England), *Westmorland*, 1936

Sackville-West, Vita, *Passenger to Teheran*, 1929

Sackville-West, Vita, *In Your Garden*, 1957

Scott-James, Anne, *Sissinghurst*, 1975

Shuffrey, L.A., *The English Fireplace and its Accessories,* 1912

Strong, Roy, *The Rennaissance Garden in England,* 1979

Thomas, Graham Stuart, *Plants for Ground Cover*, 1970

Thomas, Graham Stuart, *Perennial Garden Plants*, 1976

Thompson, Flora, *Lark Rise to Candleford*, 1945

Trevelyan, Sir Charles, *Wallington*, 1930

Verey, Rosemary and Lees-Milne, Avilde (editors), *The Englishman's Garden,* 1982

Following page: the nursery in July. Arthur built the new pedimented gateway into the fancy garden in 2001.

INDEX

ACKNOWLEDGEMENTS

Many names are scattered throughout this book. Their owners' skills, talents and physical efforts all helped us to realise this adventure; we will be for ever grateful to them.

In 2012 Joy Hall formally suggested that a book should be written to record our work and vision. Her idea was further pressed by Val Corbett and Tim Longville, who pointed out that if someone else takes on the garden after us, it would be important for them to have a record of why the garden was designed and planted as it is, and how it is maintained. Their argument seemed instantly sensible and we are most grateful to them.

We are also grateful to Val for her exquisite photographs and to her husband, Tony, for his great patience in translating my handwriting into legible typescript, while Tim scrutinised the text and made most helpful and perceptive suggestions.

Joy and Val also publicised the possibility of this book, with the help of a leaflet which Val produced. We are grateful to garden owners including Lord Howick of Howick Hall, Sir Humphry Wakefield of Chillingham Castle and Mr and Mrs Norton of Whalton Manor, who generously had them available for their visitors; to David Wheeler, the editor of *Hortus*, who included them in an issue of his distinguished journal; to the many other kind and supportive people who helped to distribute them; and to all those who responded to the leaflets so enthusiastically.

Over the years, articles about the garden have appeared in many newspapers and magazines, and we are grateful to all of the writers, photographers and editors involved. It is impossible to name them all, but we are particularly grateful to *Country Life*, which has featured the garden thrice, the first time when it was still young in 1992, then in 2013, and again in 2014, and to those most distinguished of photographers, Jacqui Hurst, Andrea Jones, Andrew Lawson and Karen Melvin, for their contributions to this book.

We thank Jo Christian and Gail Lynch of Pimpernel Press for publishing the book, Charles Quest-Ritson for writing the most eloquent, understanding and sympathetic of forewords, and Martin Gallagher of Zinco Design for his creative and imaginative vision.

We would also like to thank R. J. (Jack) Young, from whose long memory of country ways and from whose generosity we have benefited for over thirty years.

And finally I must thank Marjorie, who throughout 2013 kept me locked indoors to write, through one of the best of summers, while she attended to all our gardening and public duties outdoors.

PICTURE CREDITS

All photography by Val Corbett with the exception of those on the following pages:
Jacqui Hurst, 232; Andrea Jones, 242; Frank Lawley, 37, 38, 39, 40, 161; Andrew Lawson, 120;
Karen Melvin, 97, 98, 99, 118, 160, 168; *Walsall Observer* (1953), 20.
Drawings and paintings by Frank Lawley unless ascribed to Marjorie Lawley.

Following page: Marjorie's planting plans: detail of the formal garden.

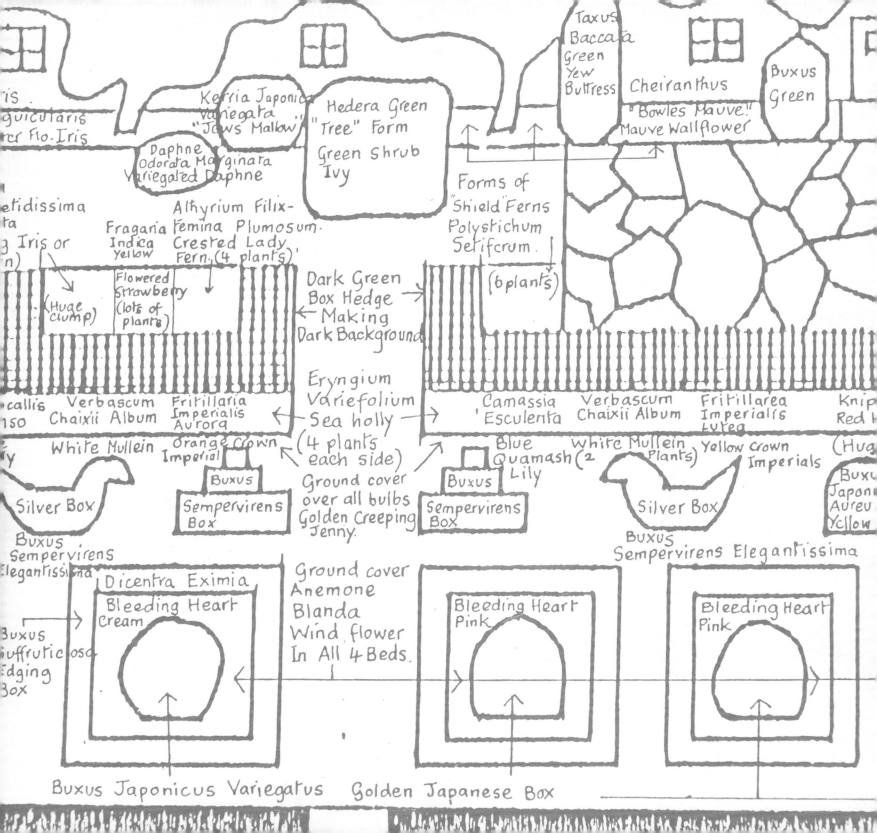

Kerria Japonica
variegata
"Jews Mallow"

Daphne
Odorata Marginata
Variegated Daphne

Hedera Green
"Tree" Form
Green Shrub
Ivy

Taxus
Baccata
Green
Yew
Buttress

Cheiranthus
"Bowles Mauve"
Mauve Wallflower

Buxus
Green

Iris
guicularis
er Flo. Iris

etidissima
ta

g Iris or
n)

Fragaria
Indica
Yellow

Athyrium Filix-
Femina Plumosum.
Crested Lady
Fern. (4 plants)

Forms of
"Shield"Ferns
Polystichum
Setifcrum.

Flowered
Strawberry
(lots of
plants)

(Huge
clump)

Dark Green
Box Hedge
← Making
Dark Background

(6 plants)

callis
150

Verbascum
Chaixii Album

Fritillaria
Imperialis
Aurora

Eryngium
Variefolium
Sea holly
(4 plants
each side)

Camassia
Esculenta

Verbascum
Chaixii Album

Fritillarea
Imperialis
Lutea

Knip
Red k

White Mullein

Orange Crown
Imperial

Buxus
Sempervirens
Box

Ground cover
over all bulbs
Golden Creeping
Jenny.

Blue
Quamash
Lily

(2

Buxus
Sempervirens
Box

White Mullein
Plants)

Silver Box

Yellow Crown
Imperials

(Hug

Silver Box

Buxus
Japoni
Aureu
Yellow

Buxus
Sempervirens
Elegantissima

Buxus
uffruticlosa
dging
Box

Dicentra Eximia
Bleeding Heart
Cream

Ground cover
Anemone
Blanda
Wind flower
In All 4 Beds.

Buxus
Sempervirens Elegantissima

Bleeding Heart
Pink

Bleeding Heart
Pink

Buxus Japonicus Variegatus   Golden Japanese Box